# E-Z RULES®

For

## THE FEDERAL RULES OF

# CIVIL PROCEDURE

*Including Selected Statutes*

BY:

## Jack S. Ezon, Esq.

and

## Jeffrey S. Dweck, Esq.

**LAW RULES PUBLISHING CORPORATION**
Old Tappan, New Jersey 07675
1999-2000
(800) 371-1271

D1548677

Library of Congress Catalog Card Number: 95-75437

ISBN # 1-887426-57-4

Printed in the United States

**LAW RULES PUBLISHING CORPORATION**
Old Tappan, New Jersey 07675

NOTE: E-Z Rules is not a substitute for the actual text of the official Federal Rules of Civil Procedure, and should not be quoted or cited to. E-Z Rules is meant to be used as a quick reference and guide to understanding The Federal Rules, and cannot completely replace them. In addition, the "overview" for each section of the Federal Rules is not meant to be a comprehensive teaching tool, as it does not consider case law. It is merely meant to provide the general scheme and remind the reader of certain key points of the Federal Rules of Civil Procedure.

*To*

*Alan, Harold, Abie, Marc, Max*
*Lee, Albert, Ralph, Carl, Danny,*
*Shweky & Elliot*

*For your support*

## IMPORTANT NOTE

All rules follow the format of the Federal Rules of Civil Procedure. Where the actual subsection letter or number of the rule is used, it is enclosed between parenthesis "( )." All other numbers and letters are produced by E-Z Rules and therefore, should not be cited to when discussing a rule. "E-Z Rules bullets" have been added in addition to the official sub-sections found in the actual code in order to make the substance more comprehensive.

For Example, in Rule 7 there are three sections, referred to in E-Z Rules as (a) - (c). These are actual sections used in the Federal Rules and may be called, for example, "subsection (a)." Under Rule 7(b)(1), however, there are items labeled "1.", "a.", and so forth. Since these are not enclosed in parenthesis, they are not the letters or numbers used by the Federal Rules.

# USING E-Z RULES FOR THE FEDERAL RULES OF CIVIL PROCEDURE

Welcome to E-Z Rules, a new way of presenting rules and laws, designed to put the "ease" into *legalese*!

E-Z Rules translates the confusing statutory language of the Federal Rules into plain and simple English. E-Z Rules are designed to give you quick access to important information you often need, without the unnecessary strain of dissecting long, monotonous, statutory texts. And remember, E-Z Rules does this WITHOUT EXCLUDING ANY KEY POINTS OF THE ACTUAL RULE OR STATUTE!

E-Z Rules is easy to use. It has been carefully tailored to meet the needs of both the law student and today's active law firm. In order to take full advantage of the E-Z Rules system, it would be beneficial to review some of its features:

- E-Z Rules is laid out so that the entire substance of a rule or statute could be grasped at a single glance.

- The rules are **boldly** titled for quick spotting.

- All rules follow the format of the Federal Rules of Civil Procedure. Where the actual subsection letter or number of the rule is used, it is enclosed between parenthesis "( )." All other numbers and letters are produced by E-Z Rules and therefore, should not be cited to when discussing a rule.

For Example, in Rule 7 there are three sections, referred to in E-Z Rules as (a) - (c). These are actual sections used in the Federal Rules and may be called, for example, "subsection (a)." Under Rule 7(b) there are 3 subsections, (1)-(3). Since these are surrounded by parentheses, these, too, may be referenced by their names (e.g. "7(b)(1)"). Under (b)(1), however, there are items labeled "1.", "a.", and so forth. Since these are not enclosed in parenthesis, they are not the letters or numbers used by the Federal Rules of Civil Procedure.

• Key words and phrases are emphasized with either **bold**, *italic*, or <u>underline</u>. This not only helps in making the rules easier to understand, but has been proven to help the user focus in on pivotal words or phrases, which may otherwise go unnoticed. In addition, certain words have been abbreviated in order to facilitate quick referencing and easier reading.

# SUMMARY TABLE OF CONTENTS

# TABLE OF ABBREVIATIONS

| | |
|---|---|
| π | Plaintiff |
| FRE | Federal Rules of Evidence |
| PJ | Personal Jurisdiction |
| SOL | Statute of Limitations |
| SMJ | Subject Matter Jurisdiction |
| SJ | Summary Judgment |
| TRO | Temporary Restraining Order |

# THE E-Z RULES ROADMAP

One of the most beneficial features of E-Z Rules is its **Roadmap to the Federal Rules of Civil Procedure.** This section consists of an overview of the key topics of the Federal Rules and the relevant rules or sections alongside. The "Roadmap" places all sections needed for a given topic at your fingertips. Please note that the overview appears in a different typeface than the text of the rule and is surrounded by a border. Also note that where only a portion of a rule is included in the overview, its title is not bolded.

The Roadmap will be most beneficial to readers who are looking to analyze problems. By using the roadmap as a checklist, it will help the reader breakdown a problem and "attack" it in a comprehensive and organized fashion and in accordance with the rules.

Studying the Roadmap will also help the reader grasp the concepts behind the Federal Rules and get an overall picture of the relevant law.

The use of the Roadmap is one of the most beneficial features of E-Z Rules, and we strongly recommend it.

13 ✓    47 ✓
14 ✓    48 ✓
19 ✓    49 ✓
20 ✓    50 ✓
22 ✓    51 ✓
24 ✓    52 ✓
25 ✓
17 ✓    54 ✓
23.1 ✓    57 ✓
23.2 ✓    58 ✓
23 ✓    59 ✓
54 ✓    69 ✓
26 ✓    70 ✓
27 ✓    60 ✓
28 ✓
29
30 ✓
31 ✓
32 ✓
33 ✓
34 ✓
35 ✓
36 ✓
37 ✓
16 ✓
41
55 ✓
68 ✓
56 ✓
38 ✓
39 ✓

# ROADMAP TO CIVIL PROCEDURE

# I. THE LITIGATION PROCESS

## A General Overview

*1. LITIGATION DECISION* - Before beginning, it is imperative that one look at a situation in light of the following:
- Is there a cause of action?
- Is there a legally cognizable claim?
- Did the victim suffer at the hands of the Defendant?
- What are the chances of succeeding, based on facts and precedent?
- *Preponderance of Evidence* - Is there enough evidence available to prove the case?
- *"Standing to Sue"* - Does the party have a legal interest in the suit?

## 2. FORUM DECISION

A. **Subject Matter Jurisdiction** (ex: exclusive, concurrent, limited, general, diversity, etc.)
- State court - Does the issue have state court jurisdiction (must look to state laws)?
- Federal court - A suit will have Federal SMJ if it is *either*:
    - A **Federal Question**
  - or • A case with **Complete Diversity**
        - There must be Diversity of Citizenship between all Plaintiffs and Defendants (Note: 2 plaintiffs or 2 Defendants may reside in the same state)
  - and • The claim must be $> \$75,000$

B. **Personal Jurisdiction** over Defendant - The court must have Personal Jurisdiction over the Defendant (see state laws and "Jurisdiction" rules below).

## 3. PLEADINGS

- **Summons and Complaint**:
  Complaint Must contain the following:
    - ALLEGATIONS - π's claims and arguments
    - RELIEF - π's relief requests
  Summons:
    - The Summons must demanding an Answer
    - The Summons must also state that if the
      summons is ignored, a default judgment
      may be entered in favor of π.

- **Filing:** Federal Rules require the π to file the
  Complaint *before* serving.

- **Service** of Summons and Complaint (see Rule 4)

- **The Answer** – Defendants have **20** or **30** days to
  Answer
    - Types of Allegations allowed in Answer
      - Deny
      - Deny knowledge or information sufficient
        to form a belief as to the truth of the
        allegation ("DKI")
      - Admit
      - Disputing Facts - partial admittance
      - *Affirmative Defense* - admitting to the
        allegations, yet including a "but"
        clause (usually claiming contributory fault)
      - Counterclaim - Defendant presents claims
        against π or third parties
      - Implead - bring in a third party
      - Motion to Dismiss (ex: *lack of claim, jurisdiction*)

# 4. PRE-TRIAL CONFERENCE, MOTIONS AND JUDGMENTS:

- **Motions** (see Rule 12):
  - Examples:
    - Motion to Dismiss
    - Motion for Summary Judgment
  - Motion Papers
    - **Notice of Motion**
    - **Affidavit** of facts
    - **Brief/Memorandum of Law** - stating legal arguments

- **Pre-Trial Judgments**:
  - Examples:
    - Summary Judgment
    - Motion to Dismiss Granted
    - Writ of Sequestration

  - Appealing Pre-Trial Judgments:
    - Final Judgment Rule (Federal): can appeal decisions *only after final judgment*
    - Interlocutory Appeal - (used in many state courts): allows appeal of motions immediately after they are granted or denied.

- **Pre-Trial Conference** (see Rule 16)

# 5. DISCOVERY

- Parties must exchange information with other parties.
- Allowable forms:
  - Depositions - oral or written
  - Interrogations - written
  - Documentation Requests

- Amended Rule 26 (1993) requires parties to make certain disclosures, while the former rule required the party seeking the information to specifically request it.

## 6. *JURY SELECTION* - *"Voir Dire"*

- **"Venire"** - potential jurors
- Once a group of potential jurors is chosen, the parties may select or eliminate jurors with or without cause:
  - Each side has limited **peremptory challenges** to eliminate jurors *without reason*
  - <u>Challenges for Cause</u>  - eliminating jurors *with reason* or based on law

## 7. *TRIAL*

- **Plaintiff's Case**
  - <u>Direct Examination</u> - π may question its witnesses
  - <u>Cross Examination</u> - Defendant may question π's witnesses
  - Re-Cross Examination is optional
  - **Objections** may be made at any time if Counsel objects to any evidence Counsel **must** *Specifically Object <u>on the RECORD</u>* for purposes of appeal
- **Defendant's Case**
  - <u>Motion For Directed Verdict</u> (Judgment "As a Matter of Law")
    - This motion may be made by the Defendant on grounds that the π's case was too weak to continue proceeding.
    - Even if the motion is denied the court may still *reserve judgment* to override the jury after trial.

- Defendant's Examination of its witnesses (to which π may cross examine)
- Both Parties may request a **Directed Verdict** before the jury makes a decision.
- **Charging the Jury** - closing comments made by the parties and the judge to instruct the jury.

## 8. VERDICT

- **General** - "Yes", "No", "Guilty", "Not Guilty" answer requested
- **Special**- the jury must answer specific questions posed by judge (i.e. telling the judge what they think the facts are)
- **JNOV** - the judge overrides the jury's decision
- **Remittitur** - the judge may reduce damages in exchange for a party's promise not to appeal

## 9. MOTION FOR A NEW TRIAL - may be granted based on:

- A Judgment Error
- or • New Evidence
- or • Jury or Attorney Misconduct
- or • Unfair Award to Plaintiff

## 10. APPEAL

- *Appellant* brings the appeal against Appellee
- Each side submits a brief describing why they should win, based on:
  - Judgmental Errors (ex: the wrong law or statute was followed)
  - Jury Problems
  - Insufficient Evidence
- The Appeals Court may **affirm, reverse** or **remand** cases back to the trial court
- If a "Writ of Certiorari" is granted a Party may appeal a case from the *Appellate Court* to the *Supreme Court.*

- Interlocutory Appeal may be granted based on a
  Motion for Lack of Jurisdiction.

## 11. *"RES JUDICATA"* - once appealed to the highest
allowable court, a case will be *closed* for good.

## 12. *PRECEDENT* - *"Stare Decisis"*
- **Lower courts** <u>must</u> follow precedents of higher
  courts
- **Higher courts**:
  - May REVERSE decisions/precedents of lower
    courts
  - May OVERRULE *itself* in a later, *factually
    similar* case.

# II. SERVICE

## OVERVIEW

- Service is the means by which the plaintiff notifies the Defendant of its impending action. Minimum Constitutional Requirements have been established to assure that the Defendant is properly notified before judgment may be taken against her.

- **Constitutional Minimum**
    - Requirements for a court to have the power to Adjudicate a case:
        - Valid service
        - "*Nexus*" - a relationship must be established between the Defendant and the Forum State (i.e. the state in which the suit is being brought must have "Jurisdiction" over the Defendant (no need to have jurisdiction over the p)).
    - **Due Process Minimum Requirements for Service**
        - "*Reasonably Calculated Notice*" (Actual notice is not necessary)
        - *Specific Circumstances* are not factors
        - Interested *Parties* must be afforded an "*Opportunity to Present Objections*"
    - Even if it is clear that Defendant has <u>no</u> chance of winning, service must be made in order to afford the Defendant a chance to negotiate a settlement. The State cannot waive service.

- Fraudulent Service:
    - People cannot be brought into a jurisdiction by fraud.
    - Service *induced* by fraud (to a Defendant <u>already</u> in the Jurisdiction) is acceptable.

- Immunity from Service:

- People making "*Special Appearances*" or "*Voluntary Appearances*" to dispute claims/jurisdiction in an unrelated case are <u>immune</u> from service, *unless*
    - A new case directly results out of the case inducing appearance
  - or • The new case involves the same subject matter
  - or • The case is a <u>criminal case</u>

- <u>Immunity Rules</u>:
    - The Court must examine the pleadings or the "surface of the suit" to establish connections between the two cases.
    - The Defendant has the burden of showing that there is <u>no</u> connection between the two cases.

RELEVANT RULES: RULE 4

# RULE 4: Summons

**(a) Summons Form:**
> 1. <u>Requirements</u> - The Summons must:
>> a. Be directed to the Defendant
>> b. Be signed by the clerk
>> c. Bear the seal of the court
>> d. Identify the name of court
>> e. Identify the names of the parties
>> f. State the name and address of the π's attorney (or π, if not represented).
>> g. Specify the time for the Defendant to appear to defend himself (before a default occurs).
>> h. Notify the Defendant that the consequence for failing to appear would be <u>default judgment</u> in favor of π.
> 2. The court may allow a summons to be amended.

**(b) Issuing the Summons:**
> 1. After the π files the complaint, he may present the summons to the clerk for a signature and seal.
> 2. If the summons is in proper form, the clerk must sign, seal, and issue it to the π for service on the Defendant.
> 3. The clerk will issue as many summonses as there are Ds.
> 4. π or π's attorney is responsible for delivering the Summons and Complaint to Defendant.

**(c) Service:**
> (1) <u>Plaintiff's Obligations:</u>
>> 1. A Summons shall be served together with a copy of the complaint.
>> 2. <u>π is responsible for service</u> (see Rule 4(m) for time limits).
>> 3. π must furnish the process server with the necessary copies of the summons and complaint.

(2) <u>Summons and Complaint</u>
    A. <u>Qualifications to Serve</u>:
        (i) Anyone *at least* <u>18 years</u> old
   and (ii) A <u>Non-Party</u> to the suit
    B. <u>U.S. Marshall to Serve</u>:
        i. π *may* request a U.S. Marshall or a specially appointed agent to serve.
        ii. π *must* request a U.S. Marshall or a specially appointed agent to serve if the π is proceeding in *forma pauperis* (pursuant to 28 USC §1915)or as a seaman.

**(d) Waiver of Service:**
    (1) A Defendant who waives service <u>does not</u> waive any objection to *venue* or *jurisdiction* of the court.

    (2) <u>Sending a Waiver of Service Notice</u>:
        i. To avoid costs, the π may notify the Defendant of the action with a *"Waiver of Service Notice"* and request that the Defendant waive service of the summons.
        ii. Any Defendant who has received a proper Waiver of Service Notice has a duty to avoid unnecessary costs of serving the summons.
        iii. If the Defendant refuses to waive good cause, the Defendant must pay the costs of service.
        iii. <u>Requirements for Waiver of Service Notice</u>:
           (A) **In Writing**:
               1. <u>Individuals</u>: Notice must be addressed directly to the Defendant.
               2. <u>Corporations/Associations</u>: Notice must be addressed to either an officer, managing/general agent, or agent appointed by law.
           (B) **First Class Mail** - π must send the notice by first class mail or other reliable means.
           (C) **Copy of Complaint:** The notice must:
               1. include a copy of the **Complaint**
          and 2. identify the **forum** (the court) in which the complaint has been filed.

      (D) **Consequences** - π must specify the consequences of compliance and of failure to comply with request (see official forms)

      (E) **Dated** - The date when the waiver request was sent must specified.

      (F) **Time Limit**

          1. π must inform the Defendant of the time limit by which the Defendant must notify π of his intention to waive service.

          2. The time limit must be at least <u>30 days</u> from the *date sent* for return (<u>60 days</u> if sent to a foreign country).

      (G) **Supplies** - must supply Defendant with:

          1. Extra copy of Notice and Request.

          2. Prepaid means of return (ex: Self-Addressed Stamped Envelope).

(3) <u>Time for Answer with Waiver:</u> Defendant may wait <u>60 days</u> after the request is sent to furnish an <u>Answer</u> (<u>90 days</u> if sent to a foreign country). Note: Although the Defendant may send an *answer* after 60 days, the response to the notice of waiver **must** still be sent within 30 days.

(4) <u>Commencement of Action with Waiver:</u> The action proceeds as normal (except for the time for filing an Answer) is considered to have started once π has filed the waiver notice with the clerk. No proof of service is needed.

(5) <u>Costs to Defendant for Denying Waiver:</u> The Defendant will be responsible for the following costs if he does not consent to the waiver of notice:

      a. Cost subsequently incurred in order to effectuate service and b. Costs of any motion needed to collect service costs, including *reasonable* attorney's fees.

**(e) Service on Individuals**: - If the Defendant does not waive service, π may serve according to:

    (1) <u>The State law for service</u> - π may rely on the state law of *either*:

        a. The state where the District Court (in which the action is being brought) is located

        or b. The state where service is being made

    or (2) <u>The federal law for service</u> - π may choose any of the following methods to serve under Federal law:

        a. **Personal Service** - π must personally serve to the individual (actual hand delivery).

        or b. **Abode Service** - to a resident in Defendant's *usual place of abode* (no business service).

        or c. **Substitute Service** - to an authorized agent.

**(f) Service Upon Individuals in a Foreign Country** - Unless waived, service may be made outside of the U.S.:

    (1) <u>By any Internationally agreed method</u> if it is *reasonably calculated to give notice* (ex: Hague Convention).

    or (2) <u>If no Internationally agreed method of service</u>, then:

        (A) Service laws of the foreign country

        or (B) As directed by a foreign authority (in response to a letter rogatory/request)

        or (C) By (unless prohibited by the foreign country):

            (i) **Personal service** - delivery to the individual of the summons and complaint

            or (ii) **Mail** - registered mail to be dispatched by the court clerk in Defendant's country.

    or (3) <u>As directed by forum court</u> (i.e. in the U.S.) as long as it is not prohibited by an international agreement.

**(g) Service upon Infants/Incompetents** - Use State law (if outside of U.S., refer to 4(f)).

**(h) Service on Corporations/Associations:**
  i. Applicability: This subsection applies
    a. Unless another federal law provides otherwise.
   and b. If the Defendant is *either:*
      1. A Domestic or Foreign Corporation
     or 2. A Partnership
     or 3. An unincorporated association subject to suit under a
       common name
   and c. A Waiver of Service has not been obtained and filed.
  ii. Service under this subsection shall be effective when:
    (1) State law is followed (as per Rule 4(e)(1))
   or (2) If the Defendant is a Foreign Corporation, and Rule 4(f)
     was used
   or 3. Delivering a copy to an *authorized* **General Agent**,
     **Officer**, or **Manager** (and mailing a copy to the Defendant if the
     statute so requires).

**(i) Service Upon the United States**
  (1) Effective Service
    (a) Delivering to:
      1. The U.S. attorney for the forum district
     or 2. The U.S. attorney's assistant or clerk
     or 3. Registered or certified mailing to civil process clerk
   and (b) Sending a Registered or Certified mailing to the U.S.
     Attorney General
   and (c) Delivering a copy to an officer or agency, if a U.S. agency
     or officer is involved
  (2) To a U.S. Agency - Delivery and Certified Mail to an
    officer/agency
  (3) *Reasonable time* is allowed for 4(i) service

**(j) Service Upon Foreign, State, or Local Governments:**
  (1) Foreign State, Political Subdivision, etc.: Service is made
    pursuant to 28 USC §1608.
  (2) U.S./State/Municipal Corporation or Organization *either*:
    a. Serve the CEO
    *or* b. Use state law service

**(k) Territorial Limits of Effective Service**
    (1) Service of a summons or filing of a 4(e) waiver is sufficient to establish **Personal Jurisdiction** if:
        (A) The forum district's state laws allow it.
        or (B) The Defendant is a Joined Party (as per Rule 14 and 19) and is served within <u>100 miles</u> from where the summons was issued
        or (C) The Defendant is subject to the Federal Interpleader jurisdiction (as per 28 USC §1335)
        or (D) It is authorized by a U.S. statute
    (2) Defendant <u>Not Subject to Jurisdiction of Any State:</u> A waiver of service notice or service of a summons is effective to establish personal jurisdiction if:
        a. The Defendant is not subject to the jurisdiction of any state
        and b. The exercise of jurisdiction over the Defendant is consistent with the Constitution and laws of the U.S. (ex: State Minimum Contact is greater than the Constitutional Minimum Contact)
        and c. The claims arise under Federal Law

**(l) Proof of Service** (if service is not waived):
    1. If service is not made by a U.S. Marshal, an <u>affidavit of service</u> is required as proof of service.
    2. <u>Foreign Countries:</u> Proof of service may be attained:
        a. According to treaty agreements (if served pursuant to 4(f)(1))
        or b. With a Registered Mail receipt - if mailed (pursuant to 4(f)(2),(3))
    3. Failure to prove service does not affect validity of service.
    4. A Court may allow proof of service to be amended.

**(m) Time Limit for Service**
    1. Service must be made within <u>120 days</u> after filing the complaint.
    2. If service is not made in time the case will either be:
        a. Automatically dismissed (without prejudice)
        or b. Service will be demanded within a specified time
    3. If $\pi$ shows *good cause*, the court may extend the time to serve (or the service period).
    4. This subsection does not apply to service to Foreign Persons (Rule 4(f)) or Foreign Corporations (see Rule 4(j)(1)).

**(n) Seizure of Property:**
    (1) <u>Notice</u>
        a. A court may have jurisdiction over property if a U.S. statute so provides.
        b. <u>Notice</u> to claimants of the property to be seized shall be sent, *either*:
            1. As provided by the statute
            2. By service of a summons under this rule
    (2) <u>In-Rem Jurisdiction</u>:
        a. If Personal Jurisdiction (in the district where the action is brought) over Defendant cannot be obtained with *reasonable effort* the court may assert "<u>In-Rem</u>" jurisdiction by seizing the Defendant's assets that are located in the forum district.
        b. The court must seize property according to the State law (in which the forum district court is located).

# III. JURISDICTION

## A. PERSONAL JURISDICTION

---

### OVERVIEW

A court cannot hear a case unless it has "personal" or "territorial" jurisdiction over the parties to a suit. A court may only have personal jurisdiction over a Defendant if it can establish a valid connection between the Defendant and state (Nexus). Questions on personal jurisdiction mainly arise with regard to a court's power to bind Defendants not physically present in the forum state.

### 1. In-State Personal Jurisdiction:

- Courts have jurisdiction over anything within its borders:
    - People - "*Personal Jurisdiction*" over state citizens or transient "visitors"
    - Property - "*In Rem*" Jurisdiction over owners or those using or possessing property in a state

- **Transient Jurisdiction** - A state even has jurisdiction over people visiting a state without any other contacts.

- Corporate Presence – Jurisdiction may be established by:
    - Citizenship: A Company is a Citizen of a state in which:
        - It is incorporated
        - It locates its principal Place of Business

---

or • Any state in which the Corporation
maintains enough activity to establish a
Minimum Contact (as discussed above for out of state)

## 2. Out of State Personal Jurisdiction:

In order to establish out-of state personal jurisdiction
two questions must be addressed:
- Is there a statute or rule that gives the court
jurisdiction over the parties?
- Is the exercise of personal jurisdiction
pursuant to the rule or statute constitutions?

### a. State Long- Arm Statutes:

- Courts may extend their jurisdiction beyond their
boundaries with long-arm statutes, so long as there
are some ties or "contacts" with the forum state.

- For Corporations, many states *Imply Consent* to
Nexus, appointing the *State Secretary* as *Service
Agent* when such "minimum contact" is established
(Ex: business, driving through state).

  - Corporate Presence
    - Courts always have jurisdiction over
Corporations that are "citizens" of the
forum state (i.e. the state where the court is located).
    - A Corporation is deemed to be a citizen of the
state:
      - In which it is Incorporated
      and • In which it has its Principal Place of
Business - where most activities occur,
where its headquarters are, or where it has
the greatest number of employees

b. <u>**Minimum Contacts Test**</u>:

The "*Constitutional Minimum*" must be satisfied whenever a Long-Arm Statute is used to establish personal jurisdiction:

      1. The Defendant has "*minimum contacts*" with the forum state

and 2. The claim arises from those contacts (with certain exceptions in special cases)

and 3. Maintaining the claim does not offend "*traditional notions of fair play and substantial justice.*"

• *Constitutional Requirement for Service of Notice:* Constitutional Due Process also requires that the Defendant receives notice and a chance to be heard, which is usually satisfied by complying with Service of Process requirements.

• Parties who conduct activities in a state accept the risk that those activities will give rise to suits, and understand that they may have to return to the state where the activity was "conducted" to defend themselves.

    • <u>Requirements to Establish a Constitutional Minimum Contact</u>:

      A Court must establish *Both*:

        • That the jurisdiction is *fair and reasonable*

and • *Purposeful Availment*

    • **Fair and Reasonable Standard**

      • The court weighs the Defendant's contact with the state and the inconvenience for Defendant to defend himself in that state.

      • Factors weighed in determining the **Fair and Reasonable Test**

        • Interest of the Forum State

        • $\pi$'s Interest in obtaining Relief

        • Most efficient resolution

        • The shared interests of several states

- Burden on the Defendant vs. the benefits the Defendant obtained from the Forum State

- **"Purposeful Availment"** is the "*Quality and Nature*" of Defendant's Contact with the state.
  - The π must show Defendant's *Purposeful Availment of the Privilege to conduct activities in the Forum State*

- **Requirements for "Purposeful Availment":**
  - **1.** *Conducting Activities within State*
    - a. The Defendant must have <u>understood</u> that its activities will "impact" the state
    - and b. The Defendant must have anticipated that its <u>*activities*</u> may lead to controversies or lawsuits
    - and c. The State has a right/interest to enforce orderly conduct
    - and d. Either
      - 1. The Defendant takes advantage of the "benefits & protection" of state
      - or 2. The Defendant must have made contact by *his own* activity
      - or 3. The Defendant solicits business
      - or 4. The Defendant signs a waiver clause to be subject to suit in that state

  - or 2. <u>Goods Placed in Stream of Commerce</u> -
    - Goods must be placed in the stream of commerce in that state.
    - Foreseeability that a product may end up in a certain state is <u>not enough</u> to establish minimum contact - the π must show that the Defendant Company's *intentional conduct* should have caused it to anticipate a lawsuit.

or **3. Harmful Activities**

- *Actual Harm* - if actual harm results in the forum state (ex: car accident), jurisdiction is established.
- *Intentionally* committing activities that the Defendant *knows* will have a harmful effect on the state will also establish jurisdiction.

- **Scope of Accountability**

  - *Specific Jurisdiction* (relationship needed) if a person:
    - Commits a Single Act (ex: car accident)
    - Transacts Occasional Business
  - *General Jurisdiction* (no relation needed) – may be established if a person/company
    - Has <u>Continuous & Systematic</u> contacts
    - or Is "<u>Doing *Substantial* Business</u>" - usually extensive facilities, contact, market directions
    - or Conducts Harmful/ Pervasive activities

- **Note:**  Most state long-arm statutes limit foreign jurisdiction beyond the Constitutional Minimum (i.e. they make it harder to establish jurisdiction)

## B. IN REM JURISDICTION:

---

### OVERVIEW ───────────────────

- Jurisdiction over property:
  - Real Property
  - Personal Property (Chattels)
  - Intangible Property

- Attachment:
  - When a Defendant is not subject to personal Jurisdiction, the Court can *sequester* property
  - The Court's power over the Defendant is limited to the value of the property
  - The Defendant is *obligated* to enter the Court's jurisdiction to defend the property (if he wants it back)
  - General Requirements for attachment:
    1. <u>Notice</u> of Attachment to Defendant
    and 2. Attachment must be by *Judicial Order*
    and 3. π must post a bond
    and 4. Opportunity for Defendant to have an *Immediate Hearing*
    and 5. Required facts/proof by plaintiff (not just conclusory evidence)
  - The Burden of proof is on the *Plaintiff* to prove that the facts warrant attachment.

- Quasi-in-Rem Jurisdiction – Jurisdiction obtained by attaching Defendant's property in the State (Note: Damages are limited to the value of the in-state property).  Quasi-in-Rem Jurisdiction is subject to:
  - **Fair and Reasonable Test / Purposeful Availment** – Expectation of being sued when the property was acquired
  - **State Interest** – Property must be "*related*" to the action in order for the state to have an interest

---

*unless* (no relationship needed if):

- In-State Service is made (i.e. Transient jurisdiction is established)
- The company engages in continuous and systematic activity/doing business (i.e. General Jurisdiction)

## C. SUBJECT MATTER JURISDICTION

---

### OVERVIEW

Aside from personal jurisdiction, the second requirement for a Federal Court to hear a case is that the court have the power to hear the kind of claim being brought (i.e. Subject-matter jurisdiction). There are two major categories of Subject-Matter jurisdiction:

1. *Federal Question*: The action involves a Federal Question

or 2. *Diversity of Citizenship*: There is both:
- Complete Diversity between the Parties
and • The amount in controversy is > $75,000

- **<u>Complete Diversity</u>**:
    - Complete Diversity is needed between ALL Defendants AND ALL Plaintiffs (Note: Plaintiffs may live in the same state as other Plaintiffs and Defendants may live in the same state as other Defendants)
    - <u>Corporate Diversity</u> (§1332): As stated above, a Corporation is deemed to be a citizen of:
        - The State of its Incorporation
        and • The State in which it maintains its Principal Place of Business
    - <u>Third Party Interpleader</u> (see below):
        - Any third party must be subject to Personal Jurisdiction
        - A third party may dissolve SMJ if it destroys the diversity requirement (ex: if the third party lives in the same state as the π)

---

RELEVANT RULES: 28 U.S.C. §1331, §1332

# §1331: Federal Questions

All civil actions *"arising under"* the U.S. Constitution, U.S. laws, or U.S. treaties have original federal jurisdiction.

# §1332: Diversity of Citizenship

(a) District courts have original jurisdiction if the matter in controversy is *greater than $75,000* is and is between *either:*
    (1) Citizens of different states
    or (2) Citizens of a state against citizens of foreign states or countries
    or (3) Citizens of different states, with additional parties from different states or countries
    or (4) Citizens of one state (or different states) against citizens of a foreign state acting as a π (pursuant to 28 USC §1603(a))

(b) If the final judgment is $75,000 or less, the court may impose costs on π.

**(c) §1332/§1441 "Citizenship"**
    1. Corporate Citizenship is considered both:
        a. The corporation's state of incorporation
        and b. The corporation's principal place of business
    2. Insurance Company's Citizenship is:
        a. Its state of incorporation
        and b. Its principal place of business
        and c. The state of the insured person (customer) if the insurance company is not joined as a Defendant.
    3. Executors/Trustees are citizens of the state of the decedent/beneficiary, with regard to related claims.
    4. Aliens are citizens of the state where they are domiciled (as per §1332(a)), if they reside there with the intention of becoming a permanent resident of U.S.

## *D. OBJECTING TO JURISDICTION*

RELEVANT RULES: RULE 12

# RULE 12:  Objections and Defenses

**(a) Time Frame for Parties to Respond**
- (1) <u>Answer and Complaint</u>: Unless a U.S. statute supersedes, the *Answer* must be served:
  - (A) *If Summons Served:* the answer must be served within 20 days after service (extended if out-of-state).
  - (B) *If Service Waived:* the answer must be served within <u>60 days</u> after request for waiver is *sent* (90 if outside of the U.S.).
- (2) <u>Cross-claims/Counterclaims</u>:
  - a. <u>Answer to a Cross-claim:</u> If the Answer is in response to a Cross-Claim, π has <u>20 days</u> from the date the cross-claim was served.
  - b. <u>Response to a Counterclaim</u>: The π shall reply to a Counterclaim:
    - 1. Within <u>20 Days</u> after service of Defendant's answer
    - 2. Within <u>20 Days</u> after service of a court order, if π's reply is ordered by the court (unless the order directs otherwise)
- (3) <u>Extension for U.S.:</u> If the U.S. is a party, it shall have <u>60 days</u> to answer.
- (4) <u>Exceptions to Time Limit:</u> The time limitations above will not apply in the following cases:
  - (A) *If a Court denies the motion or postpones disposition -* then the Answer is due within <u>10 days</u> after Court notifies of decision to proceed
  - or (B) *If a Court grants motion for a more definite statement -* then within <u>10 days</u> after receipt of π's revised pleadings

**(b) How Presented:**
  i. All Defenses must be made in answer, *except for*:
     (1) Motion for lack of <u>Subject Matter Jurisdiction</u>
     (2) Motion for lack of <u>Personal Jurisdiction</u>
     (3) Motion for <u>improper venue</u>
     (4) Motion for <u>insufficiency of process</u>
     (5) Motion for <u>insufficiency of service</u> of process
     (6) Motion for <u>failure to state a valid claim</u> upon which relief
        can be granted
     (7) Motion for <u>failure to join a party</u> under Rule 19
     8. Other defenses to claims not requiring an answer
  ii. The above defenses are made in a pre-answer motion.
  iii. <u>Implied Motion for Summary Judgment:</u>
     1. A 12(b)(6) motion shall be treated as a motion for Summary
       Judgment (as per Rule 56) if:
         a. The 12(b)(6) motion is made (failure to state a claim).
       and b. Matters outside the pleading are presented to the
         court (which are not excluded by the court).
     2. In such a case, all parties shall be given a reasonable
       opportunity to present all material pertinent to such a
       motion (as per Rule 56).
  iv. <u>Consolidated Defense:</u> All 12(b) motions must be made **before
  pleadings** if a *"consolidated defense"* is used (as per Rule 12(g),
  below).
  v. Where no response to a Pleading is requires, the above defenses
  may be made at trial.

**(c) Motion for Judgment on the Pleadings**
  1. This motion may be made after the pleadings if it does not delay
  the trial.
  2. If matters outside pleadings are presented and accepted by court,
  this becomes a Rule 56 motion for summary judgment (and all
  parties shall be given a reasonable opportunity to present all material pertinent
  to such a motion (as per Rule 56)).

**(d) Preliminary Hearings** on any motions (under 12(b)(1)-(7)) shall be
  granted upon the request of any party, unless the judge decides to
  defer the hearing until trial.

## (e) Motion for More Definite Statement:

1. This motion may be made if π's pleadings are too vague/ambiguous so that Defendant cannot reasonably frame a response.
2. The motion must point out the defects in π's pleadings.
3. If granted, the π must re-plead within <u>10 days</u> of the notice of motion (otherwise the court may strike pleadings or make any other order).

## (f) Motion to Strike - the court may order to strike something from the pleadings if it contains:

1. Insufficient defenses
2. Redundancies
3. Immaterialities
4. Scandalous matter

## (g) Consolidating Defense –

(1) A party can make a Consolidated Defense in order to join motions under this rule with any other motions available to the Defendant.

(2) If this motion is made, any available Rule 12(b) defenses that are omitted will be deemed to be <u>waived</u> (unless allowed by 12(h)).

## (h) Waiver or Preservation of Defenses –

(1) Objection to

    a. Lack of <u>Personal Jurisdiction</u> (Rule 12(b)(2))

    or b. Improper <u>Venue</u> (Rule 12(b)(3))

    or c. Insufficiency of <u>Process</u> (Rule 12(b)(4))

    or d. Insufficiency of <u>Service</u> (Rule 12(b)(5)) will be **waived** if:

        (A) Omitted from Consolidated of motions (12(g)) (i.e. if you make one, you must make all)

        or (B) Not in Responsive Pleadings, in a motion (as per 12(b)), or in an amendment (under 15(a))

(2) <u>Motions which may be made at trial or in pleadings:</u>

    a. Failure to sate a valid Claim (Rule 12(b)(6))

    b. Failure to Join a third party under Rule 19 (Rule 12(b)(7))

(3) Motion for <u>Lack of Subject Matter Jurisdiction</u> (Rule 12(b)(1)) may be made *at any time* (even after judgment).

# IV. REMOVAL TO FEDERAL COURT:

## OVERVIEW

- If a Federal Court would have Subject Matter Jurisdiction over a case, the Defendant may remove the case from state court to a federal court.
- Purpose: To prevent prejudice to Defendant in π's home state (in a diversity case)
- *"π's and Defendants shall have the option to choose Federal Courts for cases within the Federal Jurisdiction"*
- **Exception**: If **any** Defendant resides in the forum state the case may not be removed to federal court (ex: If there are 2 Defendants, and 1 Defendant resides in the forum state, the second Defendant cannot remove)
- If a diversity case has more than 1 Defendant, ALL Defendants must remove the case together
- Requesting removal doesn't create Personal Jurisdiction over the Defendant (i.e. can still argue no PJ after removal)
- Venue Transfer vs. Removal
  - Transfer - Change venue (within the same Jurisdiction)
  - Removal - Change from state court to Federal court

RELEVANT RULES: 28 U.S.C. §1441, §1445, §1446, §1447

# §1441: Cases That Can Be Removed to Federal Court

**(a) Removal From State Court by Defendant**
Whenever federal courts have <u>original jurisdiction</u>, a case may be removed from the state court <u>by the Defendant</u> (but not by the π) to the appropriate federal court in the district of original state forum.

**(b) Removable Subject Matters:**
1. <u>Any</u> **federal question** case may be removed without regard to residence of the parties
2. **Diversity cases** may be removed as long as <u>any</u> Defendant is not a citizen of the present forum.

**(c) Joinder of Cause** - When an independent federal question is joined with a non-federal subject matter, the court may choose to either:
1. Split the matters and hear only the federal element of case
or 2. Hear the entire case
or 3. Remand matters where state law predominates

**(d) Foreign State Defendant** - When a π sues a foreign state, the case may be removed by the foreign state (and tried without a jury; limitations of §1446(b) may be enlarged).

**(e) No Need to Re-file:** The federal court to which a case is removed may still hear a case that the state court had no jurisdiction over (the case need not be dismissed and re-filed in federal court).

# §1445: Non-Removable Cases

The following cases <u>may not</u> be removed:
(a) Railroad cases (pursuant to 45 USC §51-60)
(b) Common carriers if the amount is *greater than or equal to* $10,000 (pursuant to 45 USC §11707)
(c) State Worker's Compensation law cases

# §1446: Procedure for Removal

**(a) Filing** - Must file pursuant to Rule 11, with a:
  (1) Short statement of the grounds for removal
  (2) Copy of process and pleadings
  (3) Copy of orders served upon the Defendant

**(b) Limitations**
  1. Must file within <u>30 days</u> after (the shorter of):
      a. Defendant's receipt of π's initial pleadings
      b. Service of the summons, if pleadings are not required to be served
  2. If π amends the pleadings (making the case removable) the Defendant may file for removal within <u>30 days</u> after π's amended pleadings are filed and delivered.

\* \* \*

(d) Promptly after filing, the Defendant shall give <u>written notice</u> to all parties and shall file a copy with the clerk. Once the state court is notified, the state court *automatically* loses control.

(e) If a Defendant has actual custody of process issued by the state court, the district court shall issue its <u>writ of habeas corpus</u>, and the marshal shall take the Defendant into his custody, and deliver a copy of the writ to the clerk of the state court.

# §1447: Procedure After Removal

(a) A court may do "anything" to bring all parties before it.

(b) <u>District Court may</u>:
> 1. Require the party asking for removal to file all records of the state court proceedings with the district court clerk.
> and 2. Cause all records to be brought before it by having the state court issue a <u>Writ of Certiorari</u>.

**(c) Motion to Remand** (for a defect in removal procedure)
> 1. A motion to remand (back to state court) may be made by π.
> 2. The motion must be within <u>30 days</u> of the §1446 filing of notice.
> 3. If the district court lacks subject matter jurisdiction at any time before judgment, the case can be remanded to state court.
> 4. Orders remanding a case back to the state may require payment of expenses associated with removal.
> 5. The state court shall proceed with the case once the district court clerk mails a certified copy of the order of remand.

(d) An order to remand is not appealable (unless removed pursuant to §1443).

(e) If, after removal, the π joins other Defendants that destroy subject matter jurisdiction (i.e. no more complete diversity), the court may:
> 1. Deny the joinder
> or 2. Remand the case to state court

# *V. PENDANT JURISDICTION*

---

## *OVERVIEW*

- When a case is moved to a Federal Court under §1441 and the federal claim is dropped (or because "Interpleader" of a third party dissolves Diversity), the court may be *remanded* the case to the state court *or dismiss it* - *without prejudice*
    - §1367 allows the court to retain federal jurisdiction if the federal question is dropped, as long as the Diversity requirements are still met.
    - Courts have the discretion to remand or keep a *"Pendant Jurisdiction Case"* based on:
        - Judicial efficiency - economy
        - Conveniences
        - Fairness
        - Comity (prevents state prejudice against π)

---

RELEVANT RULES: 28 U.S.C. §1367

# §1367: Supplemental Jurisdiction
**(Over subsequent parties or actions)**

**(a) "Supplemental Jurisdiction"** - includes jurisdiction over any claims *related* to the claims in an action which form the *same case or controversy* (including joinder or intervention of claims).

**(b) Supplemental-Diversity Jurisdiction** - When courts have Subject Matter Jurisdiction based only on diversity, <u>complete diversity</u> <u>must</u> be continued for all counter- claims against third parties.

**(c) Court's Discretion** - A Court may decline Supplemental Jurisdiction if:
      1. The claim raises a novel or complex issue of state law
    or 2. The claim is *"substantially"* predominant over the original [federal] claim.
    or 3. The court dismissed all claims having Subject Matter Jurisdiction
    or 4. Exceptional circumstances compel the federal court to decline jurisdiction.

**(d) Statute of Limitations** - is tolled while
      1. The supplemental claim is pending
    or 2. For a period of <u>30 days</u> after its dismissal *unless* state law provides for a longer tolling period.

**(e) "State"** includes the District of Columbia, Puerto Rico, and any other U.S. territory.

# *VI. VENUE*

---

**OVERVIEW** ————————————————————

Once it is decided that the federal court system can hear a case, it must be decided which particular courts within that system can hear a case.

- Venue rules are mostly statutory, and may differ in different types of cases with a special statute (ex: FTC cases and Federal Securities claims)
- The general Federal Venue Statute (§1391) established venue for claims not covered by a special statute.
- <u>Proper venue depends on the type of SMJ the Federal Court has</u>:

    - **Diversity Jurisdiction**: In a Diversity Jurisdiction case, proper venue will be:
        1. Where the Defendant resides (if all Defendants reside in one state)
        or 2. Where Substantial events occurred or where the subject property is located (i.e. there is enough property/activity to ensure a relationship between the cause of action and the Court)
        or 3. Any district which has Personal Jurisdiction over the Defendants when the action is brought (if there is no other district) ("Fallback Provision")

    - **Federal Question**: In a Diversity Jurisdiction case, proper venue will be:
        1. Where the Defendant resides (if all Defendants reside in one state)
        or 2. Where Substantial events occurred or where the property is located (i.e. there is enough property/activity to ensure a relationship between the cause of action and the Court)
        or 3. In any district where Defendant may be

---

found ("Fallback Provision")

- **Corporate Defendants**: Any district where they are subject to Personal Jurisdiction (i.e. minimum contact must be established)

- π's often choose districts based on the type of jury (ex: large cities tend to give greater awards than suburbs, how judges are assigned, and other factors).

- <u>Waiving Venue</u> (§1406/Rule 12)
  - A Rule 12(b)(3) motion for improper venue must be made *either*:
    - 1. *Before the answer is sent*
    - or 2. *In the answer itself*
  - §1406 prevents jurisdiction from being destroyed if the parties do not object to venue.

- <u>Forum Non Conviens</u> (§1404)
  - A party can *transfer* a case from one District Court to another for convenience of the parties or witnesses.
  - A Case may only be transferred to a court "*where it might have been brought originally*"
  - <u>Transfer Discretionary</u>- A District Court is not forced to hear a case when the original court agrees to transfer a case to it.
  - The π's choice of forum shall *rarely be disturbed*, but the court must waive venue if the forum prejudices Defendant.

  - <u>Factors Considered To Dismiss a case for Forum Non-Conviens</u>:
  - If the "*ends of justice*" strongly militate in favor of removing
  - If there is an <u>*alternative*</u> forum in the U.S. or the Defendant consents to go elsewhere

- <u>Other Factors</u>:
  - Parties' residences
  - Situs of cause of action
  - Location of witnesses
  - Economic burden of increased litigation
  - Ease of access to sources of proof
  - Enforceability of judgment
  - Public Policy
    - Court congestion
    - Interest to the state/district
    - Public vs. private interests

- If π or Defendant makes Motion to Transfer Venue, the original state's law still applies

- Favorability of laws is not considered in Forum Non-Conviens, unless the new forum would be completely inadequate (ex: if the new forum would be in Iran).

- **Diversity and Venue**
  - Defendants must reside in the same state if the Defendants' residence will be the basis of establishing proper venue.
  - If Defendants reside in different states, π must sue in the district where substantial actions related to the case occurred.
  - If most events occurred outside the US, then:
    - π may bring the suit wherever there is common Personal Jurisdiction over all Defendants
    - or π may bring 2 separate cases (one for each Defendant)

RELEVANT RULES: 28 U.S.C. §1391, §1392, §1404, §1406
RULE 12(b)(3), RULE 12(g), RULE 12(h)

# §1391: Venue

**(a) Diversity Case:** If a case has federal jurisdiction based <u>solely</u> on diversity, it may be brought:

    1. In the district court where <u>any</u> Defendant resides, if all Defendants reside in same state.

  or 2. In the district court where *substantial* <u>events</u> or <u>property</u> is located.

  or 3. If no other district can hear the case, then it may be heard wherever <u>all</u> Defendants are subject to personal jurisdiction at the commencement of the action (if no such place is available, the parties must bring separate suits).

**(b) Jurisdiction Not Based Solely on Diversity:** Suits involving a **federal question** (as defined in §1331) may be brought:

    1. In the district court where <u>any</u> Defendant resides, if all Defendants reside in same state

  or 2. In the district court where *substantial* <u>events</u> or <u>property</u> is located

  or 3. If no other district is available, then the suit may be brought wherever <u>any</u> one Defendant may be found.

**(c) Corporate Venue:**

    1. Wherever a corporation is subject to personal jurisdiction at commencement of the action (any district where "contacts" would give the corporation personal jurisdiction (under the "minimum contacts test")).

    2. If none available, look to the district with the most *"significant"* contacts.

    3. If there is no one particular district in the state in which the company has enough contacts for personal jurisdiction, but the state <u>as a whole</u> "qualifies" (under the "minimum contacts test"), the entire state is considered to have personal jurisdiction over the Defendant corporation.

**(d) Venue of an Alien:** An alien may be sued in any district.

**(e) Venue for an Officer or Employee of the U.S.**

    (1) Where a <u>Defendant resides</u> (if all Defendants reside in the same state).

(2) Where *substantial* <u>events</u> or <u>property</u> exist

(3) If no real property is involved, then where the $\pi$ <u>resides</u>

**(f) Venue for a Suit Against a Foreign State** (as defined in §1603(a)):
1. Where *substantial* <u>events</u> or <u>property</u> exist
2. Where the vessel or cargo is situated
3. Wherever the agency is licensed to do business (or actually does business)

# §1392: Multiple Districts

If Defendants reside or have property located in more than 1 district, $\pi$ can bring the action in any of those districts.

# §1404: Change of Venue

(a)   i. Change of venue may be made for the following reasons:
1. Convenience of parties
or 2. Convenience of witnesses
or 3. *"In the interest of justice"*
ii. A district may transfer a case to any other district where the case *may have been brought.*

or (b) Both parties may consent to change venue (subject to the court's discretion)

(c) A district court may order any civil action to be tried at any place within the division in which it is pending.

**(d) Definitions**:
1. **"District Court"** includes U.S. District Court for the District of the Canal Zone.
2. **"District"** includes the territorial jurisdiction of that court.

# §1406: Waiver of Venue

(a) If venue is wrong, the district court may:
    1. Dismiss the case
  or 2. Transfer the case to an appropriate district

(b) Even if a party does not make a timely and sufficient objection to venue, jurisdiction <u>will not</u> be destroyed (See Rule 12 for bringing a motion for improper venue).

# Rule 12 (b)(3) Objecting to Venue

A Motion for <u>Improper Venue</u> need not appear in the answer.

# Rule 12 (g) Consolidating Defense

(1) A party can make a Consolidated Defense in order to join motions under this rule with any other motions available to the Defendant.
(2) If this motion is made, any available Rule 12(b) defenses that are omitted will be deemed to be <u>waived</u> (unless allowed by 12(h)).

# Rule 12(h) Waiver or Preservation of Defenses

(1) Objection to
    a. Lack of <u>Personal Jurisdiction</u> (Rule 12(b)(2))
  or b. Improper <u>Venue</u> (Rule 12(b)(3))
  or c. Insufficiency of <u>Process</u> (Rule 12(b)(4))
  or d. Insufficiency of <u>Service</u> (Rule 12(b)(5)) <u>will be **waived if:**</u>
      (A) Omitted from Consolidated of motions (12(g)) (i.e. if you make one, you must make all)
      or (B) Not in Responsive Pleadings, in a motion (as per 12(b)), or in an amendment (under 15(a))
(2) <u>Motions which may be made at trial or in pleadings:</u>
    a. Failure to sate a valid Claim (Rule 12(b)(6))
    b. Failure to Join a third party under Rule 19 (Rule 12(b)(7))
(3) Motion for <u>Lack of Subject Matter Jurisdiction</u> (Rule 12(b)(1)) may be made AT ANY TIME (even after judgment).

# *VII. PLEADINGS*

## *A. GENERAL RULES OF PLEADINGS*

**OVERVIEW**——————————————————

- **Detail of Pleadings:**
  - Pleadings should briefly state claims
  - Many courts want more detailed pleadings
    - To reduce litigation/discovery costs
    - To make a Motion to Dismiss easier to bring

- **Orders:** Courts may:
  - Order the party to make a more definite statement (8(e))
  - Dismiss the claim for *failure to state a claim* (12(b)(6)) - <u>but only</u> when it is *beyond a doubt* that π has no chance of winning.
- **Burdens of Proof for Conditions:**
  - <u>Condition Subsequent</u> - Defendant has burden of proving any condition subsequent
  - <u>Condition Precedent</u> - π has burden of proving any condition precedent

## *1. Specificity:*

- Requirements for pleadings have become more liberal. Specificity is no longer needed.
- Parties need not state the actual legal claim; he may use colloquial language to describe the type of action (ex: "You're liable because your actions were reasonably foreseeable" is sufficient to assert Proximate Causation).
- The party must show that the facts set forth a claim

- <u>Basic Requirements</u> – Must include:
  - **Enough information to notify the other party**

**what to expect the suit to be so as to allow them to properly prepare an answer.**
- Allegations of fault and causation
- A valid claim - such that if all facts in the complaint were true, the pleader would win
- Specificity may be beneficial in speeding up the action (ex: Settlement, summary judgment, etc.)

## 2. *Special Matters*:

- Special Matters require more detailed pleadings:
  - Special Matters include:
    - Civil Rights Cases
    - Preexisting conditions or things difficult for **Defendants** to foresee
    - Fraud Cases (Securities)
  - Circumstances of Special Matters must be pleaded so that they provide a *factual foundation* for otherwise conclusory allegations, *especially* in hard to prove fraud cases (ex: scienter is a state of mind)
  - **Fraud Cases:** Special "*particularity*" standard is imposed in fraud cases. Level of required specificity is much higher than in ordinary cases:
    - Factual Foundation necessary
    - *Rationale*: Distrust that people will bring frivolous/false suits.
  - Special Damages (Rule 9(g))
    - Must be pleaded in the complaint
    - Especially needed if a PREEXISTING CONDITION must be proven in a particular claim (ex: must prove that Mark had a history of seizures, and drove without taking the required medication to prevent such seizures)

## 3. *Alternative Pleadings*:

Mutually exclusive alternative pleadings are allowed (ex: Stephanie didn't do it; but if Stephanie did do it, she's insane) if:

- π is <u>unsure</u> of the facts, yet can ultimately find them
- Key witnesses are unavailable (ex: they are dead)
- Complete justice can only be accomplished with such pleadings

## 4. *Answer*:

- A party has <u>20 Days</u> after the complaint was served to answer it (extended for out of state service)
- Alternatives:
  - Deny
  - Deny knowledge or information sufficient to form a belief as to the truth of the allegation ("DKI")
  - Admit
  - Disputing Facts - partial admittance
  - Affirmative Defense – admitting to the allegations, yet including a "but" clause (usually claiming contributory fault)
  - Counterclaim - Defendant presents claims against third parties
  - Implead - bring in a third party

- Denying for Lack of Knowledge or Information:
  - "DKI" is considered a denial.
  - It is insufficient (even in Good Faith) if the Defendant has control over obtaining the knowledge necessary for determining validity of an allegation.
  - Rule 11 "honesty" provisions apply. Thus, a "DKI" is not appropriate if Defendant "*should*

*have known*" of a particular fact.
- If DKI is inappropriate, the court may consider it an admission.

RELEVANT RULES: RULE 7, RULE 8, RULE 9, RULE 10

# RULE 7:   Pleadings Allowed

**(a) Pleadings:**
Allowable pleadings include:
1. The Complaint
2. The Answer
3. A Reply to a Counterclaim
4. An Answer to a Cross-claim
5. A third party complaint (if that party was not an original party under Rule 14)
6. A third party answer (if a third party complaint was served)
7. A Reply to an answer or third party answer (allowed only upon court orders)

**(b) Motions and Other Papers**
(1) Requirements for an Application for an Order:
a. Must be made in writing:
1. Writing requirement will be fulfilled if the motion is stated in a written notice of the hearing of the motion.
2. Writing requirement is not necessary if a motion is made at a hearing or trial.
b. Shall state grounds for motions with "*particularity*"
c. Shall state relief sought
(2) All rules regarding form of pleadings and captioning (numbering) of rules apply.
(3) All motions must be signed in accordance with Rule 11.

**(c) Demurrers, Pleas, etc., Abolished:**
Demurrers, pleas, and exceptions (for insufficiency of a pleading) shall not be used.

# RULE 8:  General Rules of Pleadings

**(a) Claims for Relief** - must contain:
> (1) A Short plain statement of <u>jurisdiction</u> (unless the court already has it)
> (2) A Short and plain statement that the <u>Pleader is entitled to relief</u>
> (3) <u>Relief sought</u> ("demand for judgment") -*Alternative types of relief may be demanded*

**(b) Defenses; Form of Denials**
> 1. The Pleader shall state (in plain & short terms) defenses to each claim asserted, and <u>admit</u> or <u>deny</u> the allegations
> 2. If the Pleader is without sufficient knowledge or information (to admit or deny) the Pleader may so state (a.k.a. "D.K.I."). In such a case, the court will consider it as if the Pleader *denied* the allegations.
> 3. Denials must challenge the substance of the denied allegations.
> 4. If the Pleader intends to deny only a part of an allegation, he shall specify what is true and deny only the remainder.
> 5. <u>Types of Denials which a Pleader may make</u>:
>> a. *Specific denial* - applying to only parts of the pleadings
>> or b. *Complete denial* - applying to entire complaint
>> or c. *General denial* - applying to the entire complaint, except paragraphs specified

**(c) Affirmative Defenses**
> 1. <u>Types of Affirmative Defenses</u>:

| | |
|---|---|
| a. Accord and Satisfaction | k. Estoppel |
| b. Arbitration and Award | l. Failure of Consideration |
| c. Assumption of Risk | m. Fraud |
| d. Contributory Negligence | n. Illegality |
| e. Discharge in Bankruptcy | o. Injury |
| f. Duress | p. Injury by fellow servant |
| g. Laches | q. Payment |
| h. License | r. Release |
| i. Res Judicata | s. Statute of Frauds |
| j. Waiver | t. Any other matter constituting an Avoidance or Affirmative Defense |

2. If the Pleader makes a mistake and puts Counterclaims as affirmative defenses, the Court may treat it as if it were without mistakes.

### (d) Effect of Failure to Deny

1. Any denials omitted are deemed to have been admitted, unless:
   - a. A responsive pleading was not required
   - or b. The omission involved a dispute of the amount of damages claimed
2. Any allegations to which no answer is required (or allowed) shall be taken as denied.

### (e) Consistency of Pleadings - Concise and Direct

(1) Each allegation shall be Direct and Concise (no technical forms of pleadings/motions required).

(2) A Pleader may state as many separate claims as it wants in the pleadings:
   - a. Claims may be in one count or defense, or as separate ones
   - b. A relationship between the claims is not necessary
   - c. If one statement is improper, it does not negate the entire pleading (i.e. only the improper allegation will be negated).

### (f) Construction of Pleadings: Pleadings shall be construed so as to promote *"Substantial Justice"*

# RULE 9:  Pleading Special Matters

### (a) Capacity
>  1. There is no need to show capacity or authority to sue (under Rule 17(b)), unless there is a need to show Jurisdictional capacity.
>  2. If a party wants to raise a capacity issue, it must do so in a *specific negative* allegation (which must be stated with particularity, (i.e. with a specific factual foundation)).

### (b) Fraud, Mistake, Condition of Mind –
>  1. Accusations of Fraud, Mistake - must be stated with *particularity* (i.e. with a Specific factual foundation).
>  2. Accusations of Malice, Intent, Knowledge, and Conditions of Mind - may be alleged *generally*.

### (c) Conditions Precedent:
>  1. A Denial that a Condition Precedent has not been fulfilled must be stated with *particularity*.
>  2. An allegation that a Condition Precedent was performed may be alleged *generally*.

### (d) Official Document or Act - It is sufficient to simply say that it was done in compliance with the law.

### (e) Judgment - Domestic or foreign court judgments are sufficient to aver a judgment or decision. There is no need to describe the jurisdiction of the court.

### (f) Time and Place - To test sufficiency of pleadings averments of time and place are material, and should be treated like other averments of material matter.

### (g) Special Damages - must be *specifically* stated.

### (h) Admiralty and Maritime Claims - A case that includes an admiralty or maritime claim within this subdivision is an admiralty case within 28 U.S.C. §1292(a)(3).

51

# RULE 10: Form Of Pleadings

## (a) Captions; Names of Parties
    i.  Every pleading requires a caption with:
        1. Name Of Court
        2. Title of Action
        3. File number (docket number)
        4. Type of pleading (see 7(a); ex: answer, complaint)
        5. Name of first party on each side
    ii.  If the pleading is a **complaint** it must *also* include the names of <u>all</u> parties.

## (b) Separate Statements
    1. All allegations (claims/defenses) shall be made in NUMBERED paragraphs.
    2. Each paragraph shall be limited to a single set of circumstances (or whenever needed for clarity).
    3. In later paragraphs or pleadings, paragraphs may be referred to by paragraph number.

## (c) Adoption by Reference:
    1. Statements in a pleading may be adopted by reference in:
        a. Other parts of the pleadings
     or b. In different pleadings
     or c. In motions
    2. An exhibit is a part of a pleading for all purposes.

## B. AMENDING PLEADINGS

---

### OVERVIEW

- Courts usually allow amendments to pleadings (15(a)) unless the adverse party can show that he will be prejudiced (ex: the Statute of Limitations would have barred the claim).
- The opposing party has the burden of showing that he will be prejudiced.
- Each party has 1 opportunity, *as of right,* to amend pleadings.
- Subsequent amendments must be requested from the court (*"Motion for leave to amend"*) within 20 days after service of the pleadings.
- Parties may consent to try issues not in the pleadings. They may also "imply" consent by addressing the issue outside the pleadings (at which point the issue is considered as if it were in the pleadings).

- **STATUTE OF LIMITATIONS AND RELATION BACK** (See Rule 15(c)):
    - The "*Relation Back Doctrine*" moves the effective date of the "action/amendment" back to the date of the original pleadings (within the statute of limitations).
    - Requirements:
        - Notice must be given to all potential Defendants
        - The Defendant may not be prejudiced (i.e. it *should have known* about the complaint/problem)
        - The Burden rests on the party opposing the "Relation Back" to show Prejudice
    - **Application** - The Relation Back Doctrine applies only if:
        - Notice of the claim is given to the party
        - or • If misnamed Parties were used

---

- Relation Back will be allowed if a Master-Servant or Invitor-Invitee relationship exists

  or
- If the parties are Co-tortfeasors (then they must be individually named and informed before the Statute of Limitations runs out)

- Some states allow "Doe" pleadings (ex: the pleadings say Mark Smith v. Doe)


- **Acceptable Notice:**
  - The SOL may be extended with the *Court's discretion* if the Defendant is aware that the claim is being made (or should have known that it is being made) against it before the SOL runs out;
  - If the Defendant is a complete stranger to the case, the SOL runs as normal

RELEVANT RULES: RULE 15

# RULE 15: Amending Pleadings

**(a) Amendments:**
1. Parties have a *right* to <u>1 amendment</u>:
   a. Before the answer or responding pleading is served.
   b. In a non-responsive pleading, <u>20 days</u> after the pleading is served.
2. Otherwise, amending party must:
   a. Request a *"leave of court"* to amend the pleading (Court must consent when "*justice so requires*")
   or b. Obtain <u>written consent</u> from the adverse parties
3. <u>Answering Amendments:</u> - must be done within the LONGER of:
   a. <u>10 days</u> after service of the amendment
   or b. The time remaining within the original 20 day response period (from the initial pleading)

**(b) Amendments to Conform to the Evidence**
1. Issues _expressly_ or _implicitly_ consented to by parties are considered to have been raised in pleadings (although they never were).
2. Parties may raise a _Motion to Amend_ the Pleadings (to conform to the evidence) at any time, <u>even after judgment.</u>
3. If a party objects to <u>amendments, new evidence,</u> or <u>issues not explicitly included in pleadings</u>, the court may still grant/allow if it will _promote justice_ (and the other party cannot show prejudice).
4. The court may grant a continuance to allow the objecting party to meet the evidence.

**(c) Relation Back of Amendments:** Amendments will be considered to relate back to date of the original pleading if:
    (1) <u>Permitted by the law</u> providing for the Statute of Limitations in the case.
  or (2) They are <u>related to the original claims</u> (i.e. arising out of the same conduct, transaction, or occurrence)
  or (3) There were <u>misidentified parties</u> in original claim. Such amendments will relate back to date of pleading only upon reasonable notice **IF:**
      (A) A Party has received notice of the action and will not be prejudiced in maintaining a defense on the merits.
    and (B) The Party knew or should have known that the action would have been taken against her, _but for_ the fact that there was a mistake as to her actual identity.

**(d) Supplemental Pleadings –**
1. Upon Motion, Pleadings may be <u>amended for</u> <u>events</u> occurring _after_ service of the original pleadings if:
    a. Reasonable notice is given
    and b. The terms are just
2. Supplemental Pleadings must set forth the transactions or events that have happened since the date of the original pleading was drafted.
3. Permission to supplement a pleading may be granted, even though the original pleading has a defective statement claiming relief or defense.
4. If the court deems it advisable, it may order the opposing party to respond within a specified time.

## C. DEFENSES AND OBJECTIONS

# RULE 12: Objections and Defenses

**(a) Time Frame for Parties to Respond**
   (1) <u>Answer and Complaint</u>: Unless a U.S. statute supersedes, the *Answer* must be served:
      (A) *If Summons Served:* the answer must be served within 20 days after service (extended if out-of-state).
      (B) *If Service Waived:* the answer must be served within <u>60 days</u> after request for waiver is *sent* (90 if outside of the U.S.).
   (2) <u>Cross-claims/Counterclaims</u>:
      a. <u>Answer to a Cross-claim</u>: If the Answer is in response to a Cross-Claim, π has <u>20 days</u> from the date the cross-claim was served.
      b. <u>Response to a Counterclaim</u>: The π shall reply to a Counterclaim:
         1. Within <u>20 Days</u> after service of Defendant's answer
         2. Within <u>20 Days</u> after service of a court order, if π's reply is ordered by the court (unless the order directs otherwise)
   (3) <u>Extension for U.S.:</u> If the U.S. is a party, it shall have <u>60 days</u> to answer.
   (4) <u>Exceptions to Time Limit:</u> The time limitations above will not apply in the following cases:
      (A) *If a Court denies the motion or postpones disposition* - then the Answer is due within <u>10 days</u> after Court notifies of decision to proceed
   or (B) *If a Court grants motion for a more definite statement* - then within <u>10 days</u> after receipt of π's revised pleadings

**(b) How Presented:**
    i. All Defenses must be made in answer, *except for*:
        (1) Motion for lack of <u>Subject Matter Jurisdiction</u>
        (2) Motion for lack of <u>Personal Jurisdiction</u>
        (3) Motion for <u>improper venue</u>
        (4) Motion for <u>insufficiency of process</u>
        (5) Motion for <u>insufficiency of service</u> of process
        (6) Motion for <u>failure to state a valid claim</u> upon which relief
            can be granted
        (7) Motion for <u>failure to join a party</u> under Rule 19
        8. Other defenses to claims not requiring an answer
    ii. The above defenses are made in a pre-answer motion.
    iii. <u>Implied Motion for Summary Judgment:</u>
        1. A 12(b)(6) motion shall be treated as a motion for Summary
          Judgment (as per Rule 56) if:
            a. The 12(b)(6) motion is made (failure to state a claim).
        and b. Matters outside the pleading are presented to the
            court (which are not excluded by the court).
        2. In such a case, all parties shall be given a reasonable
          opportunity to present all material pertinent to such a
          motion (as per Rule 56).
    iv. <u>Consolidated Defense:</u> All 12(b) motions must be made **before**
      **pleadings** if a *"consolidated defense"* is used (as per Rule 12(g),
      below).
    v. Where no response to a Pleading is requires, the above defenses
      may be made at trial.

**(c) Motion for Judgment on the Pleadings**
    1. This motion may be made after the pleadings if it does not delay
      the trial.
    2. If matters outside pleadings are presented and accepted by court,
      this becomes a Rule 56 motion for summary judgment (and all
      parties shall be given a reasonable opportunity to present all material pertinent
      to such a motion (as per Rule 56)).

**(d) Preliminary Hearings** on any motions (under 12(b)(1)-(7)) shall be
    granted upon the request of any party, unless the judge decides to
    defer the hearing until trial.

**(e) Motion for More Definite Statement:**
  1. This motion may be made if π's pleadings are too vague/ambiguous so that Defendant cannot reasonably frame a response.
  2. The motion must point out the defects in π's pleadings.
  3. If granted, the π must re-plead within <u>10 days</u> of the notice of motion (otherwise the court may strike pleadings or make any other order).

**(f) Motion to Strike** - the court may order to Strike something from the pleadings if it contains:
  1. Insufficient defenses
  2. Redundancies
  3. Immaterialities
  4. Scandalous matter

**(g) Consolidating Defense**
  (1) A party can make a Consolidated Defense in order to join motions under this rule with any other motions available to the Defendant.
  (2) If this motion is made, any available Rule 12(b) defenses that are omitted will be deemed to be <u>waived</u> (unless allowed by 12(h)).

**(h) Waiver or Preservation of Defenses**
  (1) Objection to
    a. Lack of <u>Personal Jurisdiction</u> (Rule 12(b)(2))
    or b. Improper <u>Venue</u> (Rule 12(b)(3))
    or c. Insufficiency of <u>Process</u> (Rule 12(b)(4))
    or d. Insufficiency of <u>Service</u> (Rule 12(b)(5)) <u>will be **waived if:**</u>
        (A) Omitted from Consolidated of motions (12(g)) (i.e. if you make one, you must make all)
        or (B) Not in Responsive Pleadings, in a motion (as per 12(b)), or in an amendment (under 15(a))
  (2) <u>Motions which may be made at trial or in pleadings:</u>
    a. Failure to sate a valid Claim (Rule 12(b)(6))
    b. Failure to Join a third party under Rule 19 (Rule 12(b)(7))
  (3) Motion for <u>Lack of Subject Matter Jurisdiction</u> (Rule 12(b)(1)) may be made AT ANY TIME (even after judgment).

## D. SANCTIONS FOR IMPROPER PLEADINGS:

---

### OVERVIEW

- Rule 11 Duties:
  - **Duty to Investigate**: $\pi$'s attorney has the duty to investigate the legitimacy of a claim before filing/signing a pleading.
  - **Duty to Mitigate**: If $\pi$ is suing for lawyers' fees, he has a duty to mitigate by *attempting to dismiss* the case early on.
- Requirements for Sanctions
  - $\pi$ attempts to bring a *frivolous suit*
  - or • $\pi$ brings insubstantial claims to court
- The court can impose Rule 11 sanctions even if $\pi$ moves to dismiss the case, since $\pi$'s dismissal does not terminate the Court's power over the case (see Rule 41).
- Review of Rule 11 Decisions:
- Appellate Court's should use either:
  - Abuse of Discretion standard to see if the evidence is grossly misinterpreted
  - or • Error of Law Standard
- The Appellate Court shall not dispute whether the District Court was correct in determining facts applicable to Rule 11.
- Only attorneys fees incurred while the case is in the District Court are recoupable (not appellate fees)

---

RELEVANT RULES: RULE 11

# RULE 11:  Signing Pleadings

## (a) Signature
1. The lawyer must make signature; if there is no lawyer, the pleader must sign.
2. The signer must include his address and telephone number.
3. There is no need to accompany pleadings with an affidavit (unless specifically provided for by another rule or statute)
4. If the signature is missing, the court may *strike* the pleadings, unless it is signed promptly after such omission is brought to the pleader's attention.

## (b) Representations to Court
A signature implies that, to best of the signer's knowledge, with *reasonable inquiry*, the pleading is:
- (1) Made with a Proper Purpose - not to harass or cause unnecessary cost or delay
- and (2) Warranted by *Existing Law* (or a non-frivolous argument to change existing law)
- and (3) Well grounded in fact - likely to be reasonably supported by facts
- and (4) Based on Evidence - Denials of factual contentions are based on evidence or reasonably based on lack of belief/information.

## (c) Sanctions - If Rule 11(b) is violated, the court may impose sanctions to lawyers/signers:
### (1) How Sanctions are Initiated:
#### (A) By Motion:
1. Motion for Sanctions must be made separately from other motions.
2. The motion must state violation of Rule 11(b).
3. The motion may only be filed if the pleading is not corrected within 21 Days of service.
4. The court may award the winner reasonable expenses and fees incurred in making or opposing the motion.
5. Law firms will be held jointly liable - *absent exceptional circumstances*.
#### (B) On Court's Initiative: If the court initiates the sanctions (by Order to Show Cause), the burden of proof will fall on the pleader to show that it is not in violation.

(2) <u>Limitation of Sanctions:</u> Sanctions shall be limited to what is *"sufficient to deter repetition"* of the conduct. This may include:

    i. Non-monetary damages (ex: Equitable damages)

    ii. Penalties paid to the court

    iii. Payment of another party's expenses/lawyer's fees

    iv. <u>Money damages shall not be awarded for:</u>

        (A) Violations of 11(b)(2) (pleading not warranted by law) against represented party

        (B) When initiated by Court (Rule 11(c)(1)(B)), unless the Court issues an Order to Show Cause *before* either:

            1. A Voluntary (made by or against a party (or attorney) to be sanctioned) Dismissal

          or 2. A Settlement of Claims (made by or against a party (or attorney) to be sanctioned)

(3) <u>Order:</u> Court shall prescribe conduct and basis for sanction.

**(d) Inapplicability to Discovery** - Rule 11 does not apply to:

    1. Disclosures

    2. Discovery requests

    3. Responses

    4. Objections

    5. Motions subject to provisions in Rules 26 – 37

## E. CLASS ACTIONS

**OVERVIEW**——————————————————————

- **Certification**
    - The Lawyer representing the class must obtain Certification of a Class Action from the court with a **Motion for Class Certification**.
    - Once certification is approved, the lawyer is deemed to represent all class members (through class representation).
    - Considerations for Certification:
        - Courts are reluctant to grant certification for actions where the only one to really benefit from the case would be the lawyer.
        - Courts look to see if, after notice and distribution costs, $\pi$'s will gain anything
        - Courts examine the lawyer's proposal of notifying the class
    - Denial of a Class Action Certification motion is a final judgment, and can thus be appealed (as per 28 U.S.C. §1291).

- **Pleadings**
    - Class Action pleadings must be specific enough to be used as a Motion for Class Certification
    - The Complaint must include:
        - That $\pi$, on behalf of herself, individually, brings the suit for herself and "all others *similarly situated*"
        - The court's Subject Matter Jurisdiction
        - A definition of who is in the class
        - Substantive allegations appropriate for class certification
        - A demand for judgment (for the class)

- **<u>Notice for Rule 23(b)(3) Class Action Suits</u>**:
  - *<u>Burden of Notice</u>:*
    - π usually has the burden to give notice to the class
    - Defendants will usually only have the burden if they have a *fiduciary relationship* to the class
  - *<u>Notice Requirements</u>:*
    - Each class member shall be notified of the action and the possibility of excluding themselves from the class.
    - The court shall determine the notice requirements. It may impose a requirement of <u>individual</u> notice to all class members who can be identified through reasonable effort.
    - Notice must be given with due diligence: *Reasonably calculated* under all circumstances.

- **<u>Jurisdiction</u>:**
  - <u>Personal Jurisdiction</u>:
    - Only required over the Defendant (as per m*inimum contacts* test).
    - π need not establish Personal Jurisdiction of class members by sending a "consent" form to be a part of the suit.
  - <u>Diversity</u>:
    - Only required between class representatives and Defendant (not the entire class).
    - The amount in controversy must be > $75,000 <u>per class member</u>
  - <u>Conflict of Laws</u>:
    - Most courts will use the laws of the state in which *most* of the "harm" was done (i.e. the state that has an "interest" in the lawsuit).

RELEVANT RULES: RULE 23, RULE 23.1, RULE 23.2

# RULE 23: Class Actions

**(a) Prerequisites to a Class Action** - one or more members of a class may sue or be sued as representative parties IF:

> (1) "Numerosity": The class is so large that the joinder of all members is impracticable
>
> and (2) "Commonality": There is a common question of law or fact involved
>
> and (3) "Typicality": claims or defenses of the representative parties are typical of the rest of the class
>
> and (4) "Adequacy": The Representative parties will adequately and fairly protect the class' interests

**(b) Class Actions Maintainable:**

> i.  A Class Action will be maintained if 23(a) is satisfied, AND, _either:_
>
> > (1) Separate actions by individual members would create a risk of
> >
> > > (A) _Inconsistent/Varying adjudications_, which would establish incompatible standards of conduct for the opposing party (mostly used in property actions, nuisance, or reward cases)
> > >
> > > or (B) Adjudication for an individual member which would _substantially_ impair or impede other members from taking action or protecting themselves (mostly for declaratory judgments, injunctions)
> >
> > or (2) The opposing party has acted similarly adverse to the entire class
> >
> > or (3) The court finds that (mostly for damages)
> > > a. The facts common to class is _predominate over_ the facts specific to each individual
> > >
> > > and b. A class action would be the best way for _fair and efficient_ adjudication
>
> ii. Pertinent consideration which court must weigh:
>
> > (A) The _Interest of members_ to individually control their own cases
> >
> > (B) The _Extent and nature of litigation_ involved
> >
> > (C) The _Desirability of concentrating the litigation_ in a particular forum

64

(D) The *Difficulties likely to be encountered* in managing the class action (ex: expenses)

## (c) Order determining whether Class Action shall be maintained:
(1) <u>Certification</u>
> a. Determination of allowing a class action shall be made <u>*as soon as practicable*</u>.
> b. An order may be *conditional*, and may be later *altered or amended* before a decision is made on the merits.

(2) <u>Notice Requirements for 23(b)(3) Actions:</u>
> i. The Court shall determine the best method of notifying class members.
> ii. <u>Notice must advise each member that:</u>
>> (A) The Court will exclude the member from the class upon a member's request (before the specified date)
>> and (B) The judgment will include all members who do not request exclusion
>> and (C) Any member who does not request exclusion *may* enter an appearance through counsel.

(3) <u>Judgment</u>:
> a. *Judgments over Class Actions under <u>(b)(1) and (b)(2)</u>* - shall apply to all people that the court finds to be members of the class.
> b. *Judgments over Class Actions under <u>(b)(3)</u>* - shall apply to all people which the court finds to be members of the class if:
>> 1. The members received appropriate notice of the action
>> and 2. The members did not request exclusion from the class

(4) <u>Partial Class Actions</u> may be brought if:
> (A) The Class Action may be brought only with respect to particular issues of an action
> or (B) A class may be subdivided into subclasses (each subclass shall be treated as a separate class)

**(d) Orders in Conduct of Actions:**
   i. The court may make appropriate orders, in its discretion, to:
      (1) Prescribe measures to prevent due repetition or complication
      (2) Require specific methods of notice
      (3) Impose conditions on representative parties
      (4) Require that pleadings be amended to represent class
      (5) Determine the course of Proceedings and Procedural matters
   ii. <u>Rules:</u>
      a. Such orders may be combined with the Rule 16 provisions
      b. Such orders may be amended as court sees fit

**(e) Dismissal or Compromise** (settlement) - To dismiss or settle a class action suit, the parties must:
   1. Obtain court's approval
   and 2. Give notice to all class members (as court directs)

**(f) Appeals:**
   1. A court of appeals may permit an appeal from a district court order that grants or denies class action certification.
   2. <u>Time</u>: Application for an appeal must be made within 10 days after enty of the order denying or granting the certification.
   3. <u>Stay of Proceedings</u>: An appeal <u>does not</u> stay the District Court proceedings unless ordered by either:
      a. The district court judge
      b. The court of appeals

# RULE 23.1: Derivative Actions by Shareholders

a. In a derivative action brought by one or more shareholders to enforce a right of a corporation, shareholders must prepare a complaint, alleging that:
  (1) The π was a shareholder
      a. At the time of the transaction π is complaining about
      or b. After the transaction, and π's shares devolved on the π by operation of law
  and (2) The action is not a collusive one to confer jurisdiction in a Federal Court, in which it otherwise may NOT have such jurisdiction
      3. The efforts (if any) made by π to obtain a remedy directly with the Corp. directors/officers/shareholders *(must be stated with particularity)*.
      4. The reasons why π's efforts to remedy the situation failed

b. Derivative action may not be maintained if it appears that π does not adequately represent the interests of class (shareholders, members, and other similarly situated members).

c. Settlements and Compromises
  1. The court must approve proposed settlements
  2. Class representatives must notify the class of any settlement (notification to be given in a manner proposed by court)

# RULE 23.2: Actions Relating to Unincorporated Associations

Actions brought by or against an unincorporated associations may only be maintained if it appears that the representatives will fairly and adequately represent the entire class.

# VIII. PRETRIAL CONFERENCE

RELEVANT RULES: RULE 16

## RULE 16: Pretrial Conference

**(a) Objectives:** A Court may order (at its discretion) that parties appear for
a conference to:
    (1) Expedite disposition of an action
  or (2) Establish early controls, so that the case is not "protracted"
      from lack of management
  or (3) Discourage wasteful pre-trial activities
  or (4) Improve the quality of trial with more thorough preparation
  or (5) Facilitate Settlement of the case

**(b) Scheduling and Planning**
  1. If the court requires, the Judge shall enter a <u>Scheduling Order</u>
    (upon consultation w the parties), limiting the time to:
      (1) Join other parties and Amend pleadings
      (2) File Motions
      (3) Complete discovery
      (4) Modify:
          a. Disclosure times created in 26(f) Conference
          b. The extent of discovery permitted
      (5) Include dates for pre-trial conferences and trial dates
        (Optional)
      (6) Include any other appropriate matters under the
        circumstances
  2. The Order shall be made ASAP, AFTER the Rule 26(f)
    Conference, yet no more than:
      a. <u>120 days</u> after the complaint has been served
    and b. <u>90 days</u> after Defendant has made an appearance
  3. The Schedule may only be modified by *either* a:
      a. Leave of court
    and b. Showing of good cause
    and c. Authorization by local rule

**(c) Subjects to be Discussed at Conference** - Participants may consider and take action regarding:

(1) Formulation/Simplification of Issues to eliminate frivolous claims

(2) Necessity/Desirability of amending pleadings

(3) Possibility of obtaining Disclosure/Admissions to reduce factual disputes

(4) Avoidance of unnecessary proof of evidence and limitations of evidence (pursuant to Federal Rules of Evidence)

(5) Appropriateness/Timing of a Rule 56 Summary Judgment Motion.

(6) Control/Scheduling of discovery

(7) Identification of Witnesses/Documents

(8) Advisability of referring matters to a Magistrate

(9) Settlement and use of ADR (Alternate Dispute Resolution)

(10) Form or Substance of the pre-trial order

(11) Disposition of pending motions

(12) Need for adopting special procedures for specific complex issues (or unusual proof problems)

(13) Orders for separate trials (as per Rule 42(b))

(14) Orders to present certain evidence early (to facilitate early judgments (pursuant to Rule 50(a) and 52(c)))

(15) Orders establishing a reasonable time limit for presenting evidence

(16) Other matters to facilitate a just, speedy, inexpensive disposition of the action

17. Prepare a schedule for

    a. Exchanging briefs

    b. Further conferences

    c. Trial

18. Attempt to settle the case:

    a. The Court may require that a party or representative be present or *reasonably available* by phone (to consider settling the dispute).

    b. At least one of each party's attorney must be present at any pre-trial conference, and must have the authority to:

        1. Enter into stipulations

        2. Make admissions (regarding matter anticipated to be discussed)

## (d) Final Pretrial Conference
1. Shall be held as close to the trial date as reasonably possible.
2. Shall discuss trial plans, including admission of evidence.
3. At least one attorney per party who will be at the trial must appear.

## (e) Pretrial Orders
1. After each conference, an order shall be filed, reciting the action taken at the conference.
2. Orders may only be modified by a subsequent order.
3. Orders after a Final Pre-Trial Conference may only be modified to prevent a *manifest injustice.*

## (f) Sanctions:  Rule 37 sanctions will be invoked if:
1. A Party or its attorney fails to obey a scheduling order
2. A Party or its attorney comes unprepared to participate in the conference.
3. There is no good faith effort of participation by a party.

# IX. DISCOVERY

## A. DISCOVERY PRINCIPLES

**OVERVIEW** ———————————————————————

- Amended Rule 26 (1993) requires disclosure of certain types of materials
- All information sought must be:
    - Directed for trial
    - To establish a foundation of knowledge
- Objections to Discovery requests must specifically state:
    - Why or how the request is burdensome
  and - On what grounds it is objected to (as per Rule 26(c))

### 1. Work-Product Doctrine
- A Party may only obtain the work product of an adversary if it can prove (with facts/circumstances):
    - That such information is *either*:
        - <u>No longer available</u>
      or - <u>Unduly Burdensome</u> to re-obtain
    and - There is a <u>substantial need</u> for the information
- "*Substantial need*" and "*Undue burden*" tests may only be used when <u>written testimony</u> is received and information does not contain mental impressions.
- <u>Communications to Council</u> - can be obtained only if their essence is recorded; and only in *<u>extremely rare cases</u>*, since they clearly represent the lawyer's *privileged mental process*.
- "*Work-Product*" includes material containing:
    - Mental Impressions
  or - Conclusions
  or - Opinions
  or - Legal theories
- The <u>Work-Product Rule</u> may be <u>waived</u> when the

**main issue of the case regards**:
- Activities of Council
- or • Litigation
- or • Discovery Information
- Demand for information obtained by surveillance should be granted (although the court has discretion).

## 2. Expert Testimony:
- Rule 26(b)(4) allows parties to obtain testimony of all witnesses <u>expected to appear at trial</u>.
- <u>Non-Testimonial Witnesses</u>: Adverse parties may only obtain the testimony of witnesses <u>not</u> expected to appear at trial, if the adverse party can show "<u>Exceptional Circumstances</u>"
- Changes in Testimony
  - All changes in testimony must be disclosed to the other party before trial (Rule 26(e))
  - Changed testimony cannot be used, *unless*:
    - It is supplemented with updated information
    - and • *Notice* exists (i.e. Parties know or reasonably should know of changes in testimony)

## 3. Protective Orders
- Courts often use a <u>Balancing Test</u> in deciding whether to grant Protective Orders:

**Interests of Court in Discovery**
**v.**
**Interests Encroached Upon Party Seeking Protection**

- Tax Returns are not privileged, but have a "heightened protection" (like Work-Product)
- Upon <u>Good Cause</u>, a court may restrict dissemination of information *Only* if it is acquired through Discovery and *could not* be obtained from other sources.

## 4. Discovery Costs

- Each party bears its own discovery costs
- If Discovery is protested with *good cause*, the court may charge the adverse party if it loses.
- When using $\pi$'s employees as witnesses (from out of state), Defendant must *either*:
    - Pay for $\pi$'s employee's travel expenses
  or  - Go to the State where the employee is located

---

RELEVANT RULES: RULE 26, RULE 27, RULE 28, RULE 29, RULE 30, RULE 31, RULE 32, RULE 33

# <u>RULE 26</u>: General Provisions Governing <u>Discovery</u>

**(a) Required Disclosures** - Methods to discover:

(1) <u>Initial Disclosure</u>
    i. If local rules allow, a <u>party</u> shall provide (no request is needed):
        (A) **People** likely to have discoverable information:
            Name, address, phone (if available), and subjects of that persons knowledge
        (B) Relevant **Documents**, data, and *"tangible things"* in the <u>possession</u>, <u>custody</u>, or <u>control</u> of the party
        (C) **Materials** from which computation of damages arose, *unless* <u>privileged</u> or <u>protected</u>
        (D) **Insurance Agreements** which may indemnify or pay part of judgment
    ii. Disclosures shall be made within <u>10 days</u> after the meeting of the parties (pursuant to Rule 26(f)).
    iii. All *"reasonably available"* information must be submitted. It is <u>not</u> a valid excuse that:
        1. Investigations are not fully complete
    or 2. Opponents' discovery is insufficient
    or 3. Opponents failed to submit discovery

(2) <u>Disclosure of Expert Testimony</u>:
    (A) A party must disclose the identity of all expert witnesses who may be used at trial (to present evidence under rules 702, 703, and 705 of the Federal Rules of Evidence)
    (B) Experts must submit and sign a <u>written report</u> containing:
        1. A complete statement of *all* opinions which may be expressed at trial
    and 2. The basis and reasons for the expert's opinion
    and 3. Data and information on which the opinion is based
    and 4. Exhibits to be used to support the opinion
    and 5. Qualifications of the expert (including all publications within the past 10 years)
    and 6. Compensation to be paid for the study or testifying
    and 7. A listing of all previous cases in which the expert had testified (*either* at trial <u>or</u> deposition)

(C) The **due date** of expert disclosures is (unless the court changes):
    1. <u>Initial Expert Testimony:</u> At least <u>90 days</u> before trial
    2. <u>Rebutting Expert Testimony</u> (responding to initial testimony): Within <u>30 Days</u> of the initial expert disclosure

(3) <u>Pretrial Disclosure</u> - for any evidence to be used at trial, a party shall disclose:
    (A) The **name, address, phone** of each witness and the subject matter of their testimony (if not already provided), separately indicating which witnesses may appear trial and which may not.
    (B) **Designation** of witnesses whose testimony is expected to be by deposition.
    (C) Appropriate **identification** of each document and exhibit, and summaries of evidence
    D. <u>Other Disclosure Rules:</u>
        1. Pretrial disclosure must be submitted at least <u>30 days</u> before trial.
        2. Within <u>14 days</u> after pretrial disclosure, a party may file a list disclosing:
            (i) Any objections to the use of depositions
            (ii) Any objections to the admissibility of materials (with a reason for the objection)
        3. If objections are not made before <u>14 days</u>, they are deemed waived, unless excused for *good cause*.

(4) <u>Form of Disclosure; Filing</u> - All disclosures shall be:
    a. In writing
  and b. Signed
  and c. Served
  and d. Promptly filed in court

(5) <u>Methods to Discover Additional Matter</u> – Discovery may be obtained in *one or more* of the following ways:
    a. <u>Depositions</u> - oral or written  (Rules 27,28,30,31,32)
    b. <u>Interrogatories</u> - written  (Rule 33)
    c. <u>Production of Documents or Things</u>  (Rule 34)
    d. <u>Permission to Enter</u> - upon land or other property for inspection or other purposes
    e. <u>Examinations</u> - Physical and mental  (Rule 35)
    f. <u>Requests for Admissions</u>  (Rule 36)

## (b) Discovery Scope and Limits
### (1) In General
    a. A party may obtain discovery regarding any matter that is:
        1. Not privileged
    and 2. Relevant to the subject of the action or any party in the action
    b. If the information sought appears *reasonably calculated* to lead to the discovery of admissible evidence, there can be no grounds for objection to obtaining them.

### (2) Limitations
    a. Courts may alter these rules by setting limits on the <u>length</u> and <u>number</u> of depositions and interrogatories.
    b. Discovery shall be limited if the court determines that:
        i. The discovery sought is:
            a. unreasonably cumulative or duplicative
          or b. obtainable from a more convenient or less expensive source
      or ii. The party seeking discovery has an ample opportunity to obtain the information sought.
      or iii. Such discovery would be unduly burdensome or expensive in comparison to:
            a. The needs of the case
          or b. The amount in controversy
          or c. The limitations on the parties' resources
          or d. The importance of the issues at stake in the litigation
          or e. The likely benefit of discovery
    c. The court may act on its own initiative <u>or</u> pursuant to a motion to limit discovery.

### (3) Trial Preparation: Materials (work-product)
    a. <u>Disclosure:</u> A party may obtain discovery gathered *by another party* only upon a showing that he:
        1. Has a *"substantial need"* for the materials to prepare his case
    and 2. Cannot obtain the *"substantial equivalent"* of the materials without *"undue hardship"*
    b. Disclosure is limited to materials themselves. Courts will protect another party's work-product (ex: conclusions, theories of recovery, strategies, etc.).
    c. If a party "previously made a statement" concerning the action or subject matter, he does not have to present a new one when obtaining another party's materials.

1. <u>If the other party denies materials</u> - The party
   seeking discovery may:
      a. Move for a court order to obtain the other
         party's materials.
      and b. Apply for expenses incurred in relation to
         the motion (under Rule 37(a)(4)).
2. A "**previously made statement**" is:
      (A) A written statement signed or adopted by
         the person making it
      (B) A recorded transcript or recording of an oral
         statement by the person making the
         "showing"
d. In order to claim materials as "privileged" or to classify
   them as "trial-preparation material," a party must:
      i. Expressly claim the reason for protection
      and ii. Describe the nature of the documents and
         communications specifically enough to allow court
         to assess the applicability of the privilege or
         protection

**(4) Trial Preparation; Obtaining Expert Opinions:**
   (A) **Depositions:**
      1. Depositions of any person identified as an expert may
         be taken and may be used at trial.
      2. If an Expert Disclosure Report is required (by local
         rules), the deposition shall be conducted *after* the
         report is received.
   (B) **Other Party's Experts**:
      A party may discover known facts, or opinions of
         another party's experts (via deposition or interrogatory)
         who are <u>not</u> expected to be used at trial, but only if
         the party shows *exceptional circumstances* that
         make it impractical to obtain the expert information
         himself (i.e. by hiring his own expert).

(C) <u>The court shall require the party requesting the</u>
   <u>information to pay the following</u> (unless manifest injustice will
   result):
   (i) A reasonable fee to the expert for her time spent in
       responding to its discovery requests.
   and (ii) A reasonable portion of the expert's fee to the
       other party for the expert opinions obtained by him.

**(c) Protective Orders**
   i. Requirements for requesting a Protective Order:
      a. <u>Motion</u> for protection must be made
      b. Showing of <u>Good Cause</u>
      c. Certification of <u>Good-Faith Effort</u> or attempt to settle the
         matter without the court
   ii. A court may make any order *which justice requires* to protect
       any party from:
          a. Annoyance
       or b. Embarrassment
       or c. Oppression
       or d. Undue burden or expense
   iii. Controls which courts may use to protect parties include *one or*
        *more of the following*:
          (1) That disclosure or discovery is not to be had
          (2) Disclosure or discovery may be had only on *specified*
              *terms and conditions*
          (3) Discovery be had by a *certain method*
          (4) Discovery scope be limited to *certain matters*,
              prohibiting inquiry into other matters
          (5) Discovery be conducted in the privacy of a court
              designee
          (6) Sealed depositions only to be opened by court order
          (7) Trade secrets or confidentiality not to be revealed, or to
              be revealed in a specified manner
          (8) Parties file simultaneous specified documents and
              information in sealed envelopes to be opened with a
              court order

**(d) Sequence and Timing of Discovery**

1. Unless the court allows, a party may not seek discovery from outside sources until after a meeting of the parties (pursuant to Rule 26(f))
2. The methods of discovery may be used in any order, unless the court grants a motion based on:
   - a. Injustice
   - or b. Inconvenience of parties or witnesses
   - or c. Delays to the other party's discovery

**(e) Supplementation of Disclosures and Responses**

A party who responded to a discovery request is <u>required</u> to supplement it with new information if:
   - (1) The party learns that the disclosed information/interrogatories are *incomplete* or *incorrect*, and new information has not been made known to other the other parties during discovery (or in subsequent writings)
   - or (2) There were *incorrect* or *incomplete* depositions/interrogatories of an expert, for which reports are required (as per Rule 26(a))

**(f) Meeting of Parties:**

i. <u>Rules:</u>
   - a. Parties shall meet at least <u>14 days</u> before scheduling a Rule 16(b) conference or order
   - b. <u>Parties shall discuss:</u>
     1. The nature and basis of claim
     2. Their defenses
     3. Possibilities for a prompt settlement
     4. Disclosure arrangements and the creation of a discovery plan
   - c. Local rules may exempt the meeting

ii. <u>Discovery proposals shall include</u>:
   - (1) What changes should be made to rules
   - and (2) What subjects need discovery
   - and (3) Due dates and phases
   - and (4) Any protective orders needed

iii. All parties' attorneys are required to make a *good faith* effort in reaching an agreement.

iv. A discovery plan must be submitted within <u>10 days</u> after the meeting.

**(g) Signing of Disclosures, Discovery Requests, Responses, and Objections**
  (1) <u>Certification of Disclosures:</u>
    i. Every disclosure must be signed by at least one attorney (or the party if not represented) to be valid (recognized by the court).
    ii. The signature is a certification that to the *best of his knowledge, information, and belief* (formed after reasonable inquiry), the disclosure is <u>complete and correct</u> (as of the time it was made).

  (2) <u>Certification of Discovery Requests, Responses, or Objections:</u>
    i. Every discovery request, response, or objection must be signed by at least one attorney (or the party if not represented) to be valid (recognized by the court).
    ii. The signature is a certification that to the *best of his knowledge, information, and belief* (formed after reasonable inquiry), the request, response, or objection is:
      (A) <u>Consistent with good faith and existing law</u> (including these rules) or a good faith argument to extend, modify, or reverse an existing law
      (B) <u>Has a Proper Purpose</u> - it is not used for purposes such as harassment, delay, or to increase costs of litigation
      (C) <u>Is not unreasonable or unduly burdensome or expensive</u> when considering:
        1. The needs of the case
        and 2. The discovery already obtained in the case
        and 3. The amount in controversy
        and 4. The importance of the issues at stake in the litigation

    iii. An unsigned request, response, or objection will be stricken (unless it is signed promptly after the omission is brought to the party's attention)

(3) Sanctions:
    i. If rules are violated, appropriate sanctions (such as in Rule 11) will be imposed, either by:
        a. The court's own initiative
        or b. Motion by the opposing side
    ii. <u>Sanctions may include</u> an order to pay the amount of the reasonable expenses incurred because of the violation, including *reasonable attorney's fees.*

# RULE 27: <u>Depositions Before Action Or Pending Appeal:</u>

**(a) Before Action**
    (1) *Petition* - A person desiring to obtain testimony of any matter before an action is filed may file a petition showing:
        a. That the petitioner expects to be a party to a valid cause of action, but is unable to bring it as of yet
        b. The subject matter of the expected action
        c. The petitioner's interest in the action
        d. The facts the petitioner hopes to establish with the proposed testimony
        e. The reasons for desiring to obtain testimony
        f. The names and descriptions of expected adverse parties (and their locations)
        g. The names of the people to be examined (to testify)
        h. The subject matter of the testimony expected to be elicited
        i. A request for an order authorizing the petitioner to take depositions as testimony

    (2) *Notice and Service*
        a. After the petition filed, the petitioner shall serve a notice upon all named adverse parties, which includes:
            1. A copy of the petition
            2. A statement that the petitioner will apply to the court at the named place and time
        b. The notice must be served within <u>20 days</u> (pursuant to Rule 4(d)).
        c. If the notice cannot be served with *due diligence*, the court will:

        i. Order a specified method of publication or notice
        ii. Appoint a special attorney to represent the adverse
           parties if they do not have an attorney

(3) *Order and Examination* - If the court believes that delay of the testimony will cause an injustice, the court will:
    a. Make an order designating or describing people who
       may testify
    b. Specify the subject matter to be examined
    c. Specify method of testimony (Deposition or Interrogatories)

(4) *Use of Deposition* - A deposition may be used as testimony if:
    a. The action is related to the subject matter of the deposition
and b. It would be admissible evidence in the court of the state in
    which the deposition was taken.

**(b) Pending Appeal**
1. If a case is pending appeal, but there is a chance it will return to the district court, a party may request "leave" to take depositions for use in the event of further proceedings in the district court.

2. A <u>motion for leave to take deposition</u> must be filed, including:
    (1) The names and addresses of people to be examined and the substance of testimony expected to be elicited
and (2) The reasons for requesting advance testimony

**(c) Perpetuation by Action** - "This rule does not limit the power of a court to entertain an action to perpetuate testimony."

# RULE 28: Persons Before Whom Depositions May Be Taken

**(a) Within the United States** - Depositions may be taken before *either:*
    1. An officer "authorized to administer oaths by U.S. law"
or 2. A person appointed by the court

**(b) In Foreign Countries** - Depositions may be taken *either:*
    (1) Pursuant to any applicable treaty or convention
or (2) Pursuant to a letter of request (no need to be "rogatory")
or (3) On notice with an oath administrator authorized by U.S. law
      or the foreign country's law
or (4) With a person commissioned by the court
* * *

**(c) Disqualification for Interest** - A deposition may not be taken by any
    interested party, which includes
        1. A fiduciary, attorney, employee, or relative of a party or the
          attorney
    or 2. Someone financially interested in the action

# RULE 29: Stipulations Regarding Discovery Procedure

Unless the court otherwise mandates, parties may agree *in writing*
    to:
        (1) Provide for depositions, which may be taken before any
          person, at any time or any place.
    and (2) Modify procedures and limitations dictated by the
        Federal Rules (except extending time limits, which may only be
        extended by the court).

# RULE 30: Depositions Upon Oral Examination

**(a) When Leave Required for Depositions:**
>  (1) A party may normally take depositions of anyone *without* leave of court.
>  (2) <u>Leave of court is only required if</u>:
>> (A) The Proposed deposition will result in more than <u>10</u> depositions (under Rule 30 or 31) by a party.
>> or (B) The Person to be examined has already been deposed.
>> or (C) A party requests to take a deposition before a Rule 26(f) discovery meeting, *unless a witness is leaving the country and will not be available later*
>> or D. The person to be deposed is in prison

**(b) Notice of Examination**
>  (1) <u>General Requirements</u>
>> a. *Notice to Take Deposition:* The deposing party must give reasonable notice in writing to every other party in the action, stating:
>>> 1. The **time and place** the deposition is to be held
>>> 2. The **name and address** of each person to be examined (if known)
>>> 3. If name not known, a **general description** sufficient to identify the person or a particular class the deponent belongs to (if the name and address are unknown)
>> b. *Subpoena Duces Tecum:* If a subpoena duces tecum is to be served, notice must include the materials sought to be produced.
>  (2) <u>Method of Recording</u>
>> a. The notice shall state the method of deposition recording.
>> b. Depositions may be recorded by sound, video, or stenography.
>> c. The party taking the deposition shall bear the cost of recording.
>> d. Any party may request a transcript of a deposition.

(3) <u>Additional Recordings</u>
    a. Any party may designate another type of recording (at their expense) *in addition to* regular recording.
    b. Prior notice to the deponent and any other parties is required.

(4) <u>Deposition Requirements</u>
    i. Depositions shall be conducted before a court-appointed officer (unless the parties agree otherwise)
    ii. A deposition must begin with:
        (A) The officer's name and business address
       and (B) The date, time, and place of the deposition
       and (C) The name of the deponent
       and (D) The administration of deponent's oath
       and (E) An identification of all persons present
    iii. If the deposition is not recorded stenographically, the officer shall repeat items (A), (B), and (C) at the beginning of each new tape.
    iv. The appearance or demeanor of a deponent cannot be distorted via camera or recording techniques (ex: disguising voice).
    v. At the end of the deposition, the officer shall:
        A. Say that the deposition is complete
       and B. Explain who will take custody of the record
       and C. Discuss any pertinent matters

(5) <u>Production of Documents</u>
    Notice to a party deponent may be accompanied by a Rule 34 request for documents and tangible things (which are to be brought to the deposition).

(6) <u>Depositions of Organizations</u>
    a. A party may name a corporation or business as a deponent and reasonably describe the matters to be examined.
    b. <u>The organization must</u>:
        1. Designate one or more officers, directors, or managers to testify on its behalf
        2. Describe what each deponent will testify about
    c. A subpoena is used to notify a non-party organization
    d. An organization's representative shall testify to "*all matters known or reasonably available to the organization.*"

(7) <u>Remote Depositions:</u>
> a. Upon <u>written</u> agreement of the parties or court order, a party may use a telephone or other "remote electronic means" (ex: fax) to take a deposition.
> b. Depositions will be considered to have been taken where the deponent is located.

**(c) Examination and Cross Examinations**
1. The Examiner of a witness may proceed as provided for in the FRE Rules 103 and 615 for trial
2. The officer should put the witness under oath and record the testimony.
3. All objections regarding the following shall be noted on the record:
   > a. To the officer's qualifications
   > b. The manner of the recording
   > c. The evidence presented
   > d. Any other aspect of the examination proceeding
4. If written depositions are used, the answers shall be given to the officer (who then records them).

**(d) Schedule and Duration - Motion to Terminate or Limit Examination**
> (1) <u>Objections</u>:
> > a. Objections during the deposition shall be stated *concisely* and *objectively.*
> > b. A party may only instruct a deponent not to answer a question if it is necessary to:
> > > 1. Preserve a privilege
> > > or 2. Enforce a limitation
> > > or 3. Present a motion to terminate (as per Rule 30(d)(3))
> (2) <u>Time Limit</u>
> > a. The court may limit the time permitted to take a deposition, but it shall allow <u>extra time</u> if:
> > > 1. Extra time is needed for a *fair examination*
> > > or 2. The deponent impedes or delays the examination
> > b. The court may impose sanctions on deponents that impede or needlessly delay a deposition.

a party or deponent
...amination or change its

...ing, annoying, or

...e changes/termination.
...d until court has time to

...ask to *review* depositions

...receiving the transcript

...changes.

...position was made under
...bed

...ho shall protect it against
...ampering
...on shall be annexed to the

...t to any requesting parties
upon reasonable payment.

(2) The officer shall retain stenographic notes or copies of the deposition recording.

(3) The party taking the deposition shall give prompt notice of filing to all other parties.

### (g) Failure to Attend or Serve

(1) If a <u>serving party</u> does not attend a deposition, she is responsible for reasonable fees and expenses of the other party and the deponent, *if a court so orders.*

(2) If a <u>witness</u> does not attend because the serving party fails to serve a subpoena, the serving party must pay reasonable expenses/fees for the other party's attorney showing up, *if a court so orders.*

# RULE 31: Depositions Upon Written Questions

### (a) Notice of Serving Questions

(1) A party may normally use *written questions* for its deposition leave of court

(2) <u>Leave of court is only required if</u>:

    (A) The proposed deposition will result in more than <u>10</u> depositions (under Rules 30 and 31) by a party.

    or (B) The person to be examined has already been deposed.

    or (C) A party makes a request to take the deposition before the Rule 26(f) discovery meeting.

    or D. The person to be deposed is in prison.

(3) If a party wants to use *written questions* for its deposition, he must serve them to *every* party, stating:

    a. The name and address of person to answer them (if known)

    b. If the name is unknown, a description sufficient to describe the person or class he is a part of.

    c. The name and title of the officer taking the deposition.

4. Within <u>14 days</u> of service of questions, a party may serve **cross questions** to all other parties.

5. Within <u>7 days</u> of being served cross-questions, a party may serve **redirect questions** to all other parties.

6. Within <u>7 days</u> of redirect-questions, a party may serve **recross questions** upon all other parties.

7. Courts may change the above times for cause shown.

**(b) Officer to Prepare Record** - All questions and notices shall be copied and given to the recording officer.

**(c) Notice of Filing** - The party filing must promptly give notice of the filing to all other parties.

# RULE 32: Use of Depositions in Court

**(a) Use of Depositions** - Depositions (if admissible under the FRE) may be used in court for any of the following purposes:
  (1) To <u>contradict or impeach</u> the testimony of a deponent as a witness or other purposes allowed by the FRE.
  (2) As <u>testimony of an adverse party</u> or on behalf of an organization, *but only* to be used by an *<u>adverse</u>* party for any purpose.
  (3) As personal <u>testimony of a non-party</u> to be used by any party for any purpose, if the court finds that:
      (A) The witness is dead
      or (B) The witness is too far (more than 100 miles from the place of trial, or outside of the U.S.), unless it appears that the witness' absence was procured by a party
      or (C) The witness is sick or imprisoned
      or (D) A party offering the deposition is unable to procure attendance of the witness by subpoena
      or (E) It is "in the interest of justice" *(upon application and notice)*
  (4) If only part of the deposition is used as evidence, an adverse party may require the remainder to be shown for fairness.
  5. If a deposition is to be used against a party, the part must:
      a. Be present at time of the deposition
      or b. Have reasonable notice of the deposition
  6. A party may use depositions properly taken for another action involving the same subject.
  7. Depositions taken without leave of court <u>cannot</u> be used if:
      a. A party, with *due diligence*, is unable to obtain counsel at the deposition.
      or b. A party, with *greater than* <u>11 days</u> notice of the deposition, promptly moved for a protective order.

**(b) Objections to Admissibility** - may be made at any time during the trial or hearing.

**(c) Forms of Presentation**
    1. Depositions may be given in stenographic or non-stenographic form, unless the court rules otherwise.
    2. If non-stenographic, the party shall provide a transcript to the court.

**(d) Effect of Errors in Depositions**
    (1) <u>Notice</u> - All errors shall be deemed waived unless written objection is served promptly after the party gave notice.
    (2) <u>Disqualification of an Officer</u> - waived unless:
        a) An objection is made before the deposition
        b) An objection is made promptly after learning of the officer's disqualification
    (3) <u>Taking of Deposition</u>
        (A) *Competency of witness, relevancy, materiality of testimony* - not waived unless the objection would have definitely caused the deposition to be removed.
        (B) *Irregularities, manner of posing questions, oath affirmation, and conduct* - waived if not made promptly <u>at</u> the deposition.
        (C) *Objections to form of written questions* – waived unless objected to within <u>5 days</u> after the date that the last authorized questions were served.
    (4) <u>Completion/Return of Deposition</u>, *transcribed, certified, filed* - waived unless a motion to suppress is made within *reasonable time* (from when *due diligence* would have discovered it).

# RULE 33: Interrogatories To Parties

**(a) Availability**
    1. Interrogatories may be served to any party once service of process is properly made.
    2. A party may not serve more than 25 interrogatories
    3. Leave of court is needed if:
        a. A party wants to serve more 25 interrogatories
    or b. A party wants to serve interrogatories early

**(b) Answers and Objections**

(1) <u>Answering Interrogatories</u>:
   a. Each question, unless it is objected to, must be answered:
      1. Separately
      2. Fully
      3. In Writing
      4. Under Oath
   b. If questions are objected to, the objecting party shall state the reasons for the objection and answer those questions that are not objectionable.

(2) <u>Signatures</u>:
   a. Answers - must be signed by the person writing them
   b. Objections - must be signed by the attorney making them

(3) <u>Time Limitation</u>:
   a. Must return interrogatories within <u>30 Days</u> after they were served.
   b. The court may change this time limitation, or parties may agree to new limits.

(4) <u>Objections</u>:
   a. Grounds for objections must be stated with specificity.
   b. Any objection not *timely* stated is waived unless good cause is shown.

(5) The party submitting interrogatories may move for a Rule 37(a) order for sanctions with respect to any objection or failure to answer an interrogatory.

**(c) Use at Trial**
   1. This rule is subject to Rule 26(b) and the Federal Rules of Evidence.
   2. A court may order that an interrogatory not be answered until certain discovery has been completed.

**(d) Option to Produce Business Records** - The answering party may opt to allow a questioning party to see records and get an answer himself (thus shifting the burden and time of research, auditing, etc. to his opponent).

## B. PRODUCTION OF DOCUMENTS:

---

### OVERVIEW——————————————————

- Documents need not be in the possession of a party.  They may only be in CONTROL or CUSTODY
- Procedure for Production of International Entities:
    - The U.S. party must draft a Letter Rogatory
    - The letter must be sent to the Central Authority of the Foreign Country
    - The Letter must be forwarded to a "Domestic" court in the Foreign Jurisdiction
    - The Foreign court must send an Order of Discovery to the International party
    - **Problem:** Many countries have many more discovery limits, and can deny Americans access to information.

---

RELEVANT RULES: RULE 34

# RULE 34:  Production of Documents and Entry For Inspection

**(a) Scope** - A party may request another party to:
>    1. Produce any document or, information, in its custody (within the scope of Rule 26(b)).
>    2. Permit entry (upon notice) for inspection and surveying (within the scope of Rule 26(b)).

**(b) Procedure**
>    1. Requirements For the Request:
>        a. Must state each item or category of items (must be stated separately)
>        b. Must specify items to be inspected with *"reasonable particularity"*
>        c. Must describe the manner in which the inspection will be done
>        d. Must request a reasonable time and place for inspection
>    2. Leave of court is needed to serve requests early.
>    3. Within <u>30 Days</u> (subject to change by agreement or by the court) of the request, the party (upon whom the request was served) shall state which items are permitted and which are objected to (and reasons for any objections).

**(c) Non-Parties** - may be compelled to produce documents under Rule 45.

## C. PHYSICAL/MENTAL EXAMINATIONS:

RELEVANT RULES: RULE 35

### OVERVIEW

- Examinations may only be given to PARTIES
- Prerequisites for exam:
  - Must show <u>Good Cause</u> for requiring an exam
  - The exam must correlate to a fact *in controversy*
- An attorney may accompany clients to examinations as long as they do not interfere with the exam.
- The only basis for the exclusion of an attorney is a *"compelling showing of need."*

# RULE 35: Physical/Mental Examinations

**(a) Order of Examination**
   1. <u>Procedure</u>:
      a. Obtain a court order (by motion)
      b. Show *good cause* for the physical or mental examination
      c. Show that it is a *material matter in controversy*
   2. Must give notice to all parties, specifying the:
      a. Examiner
      b. Time and place of exam
      c. Scope of examination

**(b) Report of Examiner**
   (1) An Adverse party may request a report of the examination
   (2) By requesting a report or taking an examiner's testimony, the examined party waives the privilege to get another examiner to testify for her.
   (3) Agreements by parties may be made to alter these rules.

## D. ADMISSIONS:

---

### OVERVIEW —————————————————————————

- Admissions are obtained to *eliminate* disputed facts in trial, while interrogatories and depositions only constitute *evidence* from which to argue facts.
- A party who obtains an Admission <u>does not</u> waive his right to rely on that information if the adverse party attempts to present evidence "overlapping" or "exceeding" the admission (ex: that damages are greater than admitted).

---

RELEVANT RULES: RULE 36

# RULE 36:  Request for Admission

## (a) Request for Admission

1. A party may serve upon any other party a written request for an admission (for the pending action only) regarding statements of opinion or fact, the applicability of law to fact, and the truth of opinions, authenticity of documents, etc. (within the scope of Rule 26(b))
2. If no answer or objection is received within <u>30 Days</u> (can be changed by agreement of the parties or by the court) of the request for admission, a party is considered to admit the allegation.
3. If an objection is made, the reasons shall be stated in detail.
4. Admissions and denials must be specific to the related questions.
5. A party may not give "lack of knowledge and information" as a reason for not answering a request, unless:
    a. The party has made a reasonable inquiry
    and b. There is not enough information to enable the party to admit or deny.
6. If court does not like an objection, it can order that an answer be made (and if it is not made, the court presumes an admission).
7. Leave of court is needed for early requests.

## (b) Effect of Admission

1. Any admissions are *conclusively established*, unless the court grants a motion to <u>withdraw</u> or <u>amend</u> the admission.
2. Admissions are made only in regard to the pending action (i.e. cannot be used in other actions).
3. Amendments or withdrawals may be permitted on a showing that the *"presentation of the merits of the action will be subserved"* and if the opposing party cannot show that he will be prejudiced.

## E. SANCTIONS:

---

### OVERVIEW

- Rule 37 Sanctions should be imposed when the adverse party or the court can show that a delay/refusal of discovery was due to *either*:
    - Willfulness
    - or • Bad Faith
    - or • Any fault of party/deponent
- Inability to answer is <u>not</u> grounds for Rule 37 sanctions.
- <u>Sanctions include</u>:
    - Dismissal
    - Default Judgment
    - Admission
    - Monetary penalties
- Dismissals and default judgments are very <u>rare</u>; most Courts refuse to grant it because a party will often suffer for their attorney's inadequacy.

---

RELEVANT RULES: RULE 37

# RULE 37:  Sanctions for Failure to Cooperate in Discovery

**(a) Motion for Order Compelling Disclosure of Discovery**
  (1) Appropriate Court:
      a. *Where action pending* - motion required where deponent is a party
      b. *Where deposition is pending* - motion required if deponent is not a party
  (2) Motion:
      (A) If a party fails to disclose (under 26(a)), the court may grant a motion to compel disclosure, upon showing a *good faith* effort to obtain the discovery without the court's help.
      (B) If a deponent refuses to answer, a party may make a motion for an order compelling an answer. If the court denies the motion, the deponent may be granted a protective order (under Rule 26(c)).
  (3) Evasive or Incomplete Answer - considered a failure to answer.
  (4) Expenses and Sanctions:
      a. If the motion is **granted**, or disclosure is made after the motion is filed, the party/deponent must pay reasonable fees spent to make the motion.
      b. If the motion is **denied**, and the motion is not *substantially justified*, the party making the motion must pay reasonable fees spent to oppose the motion.
      c. If the motion is denied in part and granted in part, expenses may be reasonably apportioned.
      d. All sanctions will be determined by a court hearing.

**(b) Failure to Comply With Order**
  (1) Sanctions By Court In District Where Deposition Is Taken - Failure to be sworn or provide an answer is considered contempt in that court.
  (2) Sanctions By Court In District Where Action Is Pending - the Court may:
      (A) Conclude that matters sought to be discovered by a party are to be found in that party's favor
      (B) Refuse to allow the disobedient party to support or oppose designated claims or defenses
      (C) Render a default judgment or strike a pleading

(D) Hold the disobedient person in contempt of court (unless it is in regards to a Rule 35 examination)

(E) Require the opposing party to pay reasonable attorney's fees resulting from his disobedience, *unless* the court finds the disobedience *substantially justified.*

## (c) Failure to Disclose

(1) Penalty for a party that does not disclose information (i.e. information required under Rule 26(a)):

    a. The non-disclosing party shall not be allowed to use the undisclosed information as evidence at trial or in hearings.

and b. Sanctions may be imposed if:

    1. There is no *substantial justification* not to disclose the information

    and 2. The failure to disclose was harmful

(2) If a party refuses to admit to the authenticity of a document and another party proves its authenticity, the court may impose fees spent to prove the document's validity, *unless:*

    (A) The request was objectionable under Rule 36(a)

    or (B) The admission sought was of no substantial importance

    or (C) The party failing to admit had reasonable grounds to believe that he would prevail on that matter

    or (D) Other good cause is shown

## (d) Failure to Attend a Deposition, Serve Answers, or Respond to Production Requests - subjects a party to Rule 37(b) sanctions.

## (e) Subpoena of a Person in a Foreign Country - Abrogated

## (f) Expenses Against the United States - Repealed

## (g) Failure to Participate in Framing a Discovery Plan - If a *good faith* effort is made to agree on a 26(f) plan, reasonable attorneys fees to bring the plan to court will be imposed.

# X. SUMMARY JUDGMENT

## OVERVIEW

- Summary Judgment may be requested by either party in order to prevent a case from going to trial.
- Summary Judgment may only be granted if there is no question of fact to be determined.
- If the Summary Judgment is requested, the judge will adjudicate the case based on the applicable law and the facts as stated in the pleadings.

- **Burden of Proof:**
  - The party moving for a Summary Judgment bears the burden of proving that there is no evidence to support the non-moving party's case.
  - The non-moving party has the burden of showing that there remains a *genuine issue of material fact* which would have to be decided by a factfinder at trial.
  - Summary judgment is appropriate if only a question of law remains to be decided (i.e. the judge will make a decision as a *matter of law* since there is no need to find facts at trial)

- **Evidence:**
  - <u>Significant Probative Evidence</u>: Whenever a "fair-minded" jury could return a verdict for the non-moving party, the case should go to trial.
  - Evidence shall be viewed in a light most favorable to the non-moving party.
  - The non-moving party may <u>not</u> rely on allegations in the pleadings to defend summary judgment (i.e. it needs "<u>specific facts</u>" - and not "allegations" to defend the motion)

- **Discovery:**

  - The court is obligated to give the non-moving party an adequate opportunity for discovery (to obtain such specific facts, as required to oppose the Motion for Summary Judgment).
  - A Rule 56(f) Affidavit to extend the time for discovery must specify what the party expects to obtain from discovery, and why such information hasn't yet been obtained.

---

RELEVANT RULES: RULE 56

## RULE 56: Summary Judgment

**(a) For Claimant (π):** A party may move for summary judgment (with or without supporting affidavits) *after* either:
     1. 20 days from commencement of the action
  or 2. Service of a motion for summary judgment ("SJ") by the adverse party

**(b) For Defendant:** May move for Summary Judgment at *any time* (with or without supporting affidavits).

**(c) Motions and Proceedings**
    1. A Motion for SJ must be served to the adverse party at least 10 days before the scheduled hearings.
    2. The adverse party may serve opposing affidavits *at any time* before the hearing.
    3. Summary Judgment must be based upon:
       a. Pleadings
       b. Depositions
       c. Interrogatories
       d. Admissions
       e. Affidavits
    4. Summary Judgment shall be rendered if, based on the above:
       a. There is no *genuine issue of any material fact* shown
         (discretionary)
  and b. The moving party is entitled to judgment *as a matter of law.*

## (d) Case Not Fully Adjudicated on Motion
1. If only part of the case is adjudicated, the court shall determine which facts remain at issue for trial.
2. The Judge shall file an order establishing the "<u>adjudicated facts</u>" and how they affect the amount in controversy.

## (e) Defending Motion for SJ:
1. <u>Requirements for Affidavits</u>:
   a. Must include personal knowledge of facts (admissible under the Federal Rules of Evidence)
   b. Shall show that the affiant is competent to testify
   c. The court may permit the affidavit to be supplemented by depositions, interrogatories, or other affidavits.

2. <u>Responding to a Motion for SJ:</u>
   a. The adverse party must set forth *specific facts* showing that there is a genuine issue for trial (cannot rely on pleadings).
   b. If the adverse party cannot show that there is a genuine issue, SJ shall be entered against her *if appropriate* (given an opportunity for discovery).

## (f) When Affidavits are Unavailable
If a party opposing a motion for SJ can show in its affidavit that it cannot obtain affidavits containing facts <u>*essential*</u> to justify it's opposition to SJ, then the court may:
   1. Refuse the application for SJ
   or 2. Order a continuance to permit affidavits to be obtained (or other depositions or discovery to be had)
   or 3. Make such order as it deems just

## (g) Affidavits Made in Bad Faith (to delay the proceeding)
1. A party making an improper affidavit shall pay the other party's reasonable expenses (including attorney fees) associated with the motion for SJ.
2. The offending party or attorney may be guilty of contempt.

# XI. THIRD PARTY CLAIMS

## A. IMPLEADER AND JOINDER:

---

### OVERVIEW

- Process for Determining Necessity of Joinder
    - Courts look to see if a party can be joined under Rule 19(a)
    - If no Personal Jurisdiction can be established over the third party, the court must determine whether
        - To proceed with the case anyway (without joining the third party)
        - or To dismiss case (if the third party is indispensable to the case)
- *The rule is not to be applied in a rigid manner, but should, instead, be governed by the particularities of the individual case.*
- A party in a Joint & Several liability action is merely a "*Permissive Party*" not a Compulsory one.

- Claim Preclusion:
    - All claims related to the action must be joined (or else are forfeited)
    - Unrelated claims may be brought, but they are not precluded from future litigation.

---

RELEVANT RULES: RULE 13, RULE 14, RULE 19, RULE 20, RULE 21, RULE 18, RULE 42

# RULE 13: Counterclaims / Cross-claims

**(a) Compulsory Counterclaims**

    i. A *"Compulsory Counterclaim"* is any RELATED claim - "arising out of" the initial action *(i.e. they must arise out of the "same transaction or occurrence")*.

    ii. Compulsory Counterclaims <u>MUST</u> be joined.

    iii. Any third parties involved must have Personal Jurisdiction

    iv. The Counterclaim must be stated in the pleading *unless:*

        (1) The claim is already subject to another pending action

        (2) The Defendant brings the suit by attachment or process without the Court's jurisdiction.

**(b) Permissive Counterclaims**

    1. A *"Permissive Counterclaim"* is <u>any</u> claim *against* an *opposing party* (not a new party) which is not related to action.

    2. Permissive Counterclaims MUST BE STATED IN PLEADINGS

**(c) Counterclaims exceeding Opposing Claims** – Counterclaims may seek more relief or different relief than the original claims that the opposing party had sought.

**(d) Counterclaims against the U.S.** - These rules shall not enlarge the present limits, (fixed by statute) of asserting Counterclaims against the U.S. government.

**(e) Post-Pleading Counterclaims** - may be presented as a *Counterclaim* in a *Supplemental Pleading*, if the Court allows.

**(f) Omitted Counterclaim** - a pleader may obtain leave of court, to Counterclaim by amending the pleading, only if it is omitted by

    1. Oversight

    or 2. Inadvertence

    or 3. Excusable neglect

    or 4. *When justice so requires*.

**(g) Cross-claims against a Co-Party** -  are usually considered permissive.

    1. <u>Same Transaction</u>:  May allow Cross-claim against a co-party for a claim either:

        a. *Arising out of the same transaction or occurrence* of *either*:

            1. The original action

        or 2. A Counterclaim

        or b. Relating to any property subject to the original action

    2. <u>Indemnity</u>: Cross-claims may include a claim to a co-party to indemnify the claimant for all or part of the liability arising out of the action.

**(h) Joinder of Additional Parties** - parties may be joined in Counterclaims and Cross-claims (pursuant to Rules 19 and 20).

**(i) Separate Trials; Separate Judgments** - Judgment on a Cross-Claim or Counterclaim may be made in accordance with Rule 54(b) (even if the claims of the opposing party have been dismissed or otherwise disposed of) if:

    1. A Court orders separate trials pursuant to Rule 42(b)

    and 2. The Court has jurisdiction to do so.

# RULE 14: Third Party Practice

**(a) When Defendant may bring a third party**

1. At any time <u>after</u> the commencement of an action, the Defendant may become a "third party π" by serving a Complaint on a third party (who is not in the original action). This happens when the Defendant feels that the third party is liable to *indemnify* the Defendant for any judgment (ex: insurance company or surety).

2. If the Defendant serves the third party no later than <u>10 days</u> after serving its original Answer. No "leave of court" is needed to serve the third party. After 10 days, the Defendant must get "leave of court" by filing a motion with notice to all parties.

3. The third party is then known as a "Third Party Defendant" and the Defendant is known as a "Third Party Plaintiff."

4. Third Party Defendant's options in response to Defendant's pleadings:

   a. <u>Answer</u> - third may assert any defenses which the Defendant may have to π's claim.

   b. <u>Counterclaim against π</u> - *arising out of the same transaction or occurrence* of π's claim against Defendant.

   c. <u>Cross-claims against Defendant</u>

5. π may Counterclaim against third

6. Any party may move to:

   a. Strike third party claim

   or b. Severe the claim

   or c. Separate trial

7. A third party may implead a 4th party who may also be liable to the Defendant or the third party (Note: Complete diversity is not needed for third party.)

**(b) When π may bring a third party**: When a Counterclaim is made against the π, the π may bring in a third party just as the Defendant (under Rule 14(a)).

# RULE 19: Compulsory Joinder

**(a) Persons To Be Joined** (if feasible)
  1. <u>Requirements</u>:
      a. Joined parties must be subject to <u>Personal Jurisdiction</u>
    and b. Joinder cannot destroy SMJ (diversity)
  2. <u>A Third Party MUST be joined if</u>:
      (1) *Complete relief* cannot be accorded among the present parties without joining the third party.
    or (2) The third party claims a *related interest* in the action, and its absence from the suit may:
        (i) Impair or Impede its ability to protect that interest.
      or (ii) Leave any of the present parties subject to <u>double liability</u> or <u>inconsistent verdicts</u>.
  3. If a third party refuses to be a π, he may, upon the Court's discretion, be made:
      a. A Defendant
    or b. An *Involuntary π*
  4. If a third party objects to venue, and his presence makes venue improper, the joinder will be dismissed (and the entire case itself will also be dismissed if third party is considered an "*indispensable party*").

**(b) Determination by Court Whenever Joinder is Not Feasible**
  1. The Court may determine that a third party is "*indispensable*," and dismiss the case if he cannot be joined.
  2. An "<u>Indispensable Party</u>" is a party who in, "*in equity or in conscience*" the case should not proceed without.

  3. <u>FACTORS CONSIDERED</u> (to determine if third party is "indispensable"):
      a. The Extent of prejudices to the present Party's that the third party's absence may bring
      b. The Extent that Prejudices may be avoided or reduced by other means
      c. The Adequacy of judgment without the third party
      d. Whether the π will have an adequate remedy if the case were dismissed for non-joinder.

# RULE 20: Permissive Joinder of Parties

**(a) Permissive Joinder –**

1. All persons may join as a π or a Defendant, if they assert or are subject to any *right to relief* (ex: Indemnity) which *both*:

   a. Arises out of the same transaction or occurrence (or series of transactions or occurrences)

   and b. Has a question of law or fact common to all co-parties in the action (i.e. if you are guilty of negligence and you think a third party is contributorily negligent, you can join her).

2. There is no need for all πs or Ds to seek all claims of relief being claimed in the action; judgment will be accorded as per each party's respective rights or liabilities.

**(b) Separate Trials -** The Court may order separate trials or make *other such orders* to prevent:

1. A party from being embarrassed

or 2. Delay

or 3. Prejudice

or 4. A party from incurring undue expense from the inclusion of a third party, if no claims exists between the parties.

# RULE 21: Misjoinder and Non-Joinder of Parties

1. Misjoinder is NOT a ground for dismissal of an action.
2. Parties may be dropped or added at any stage of the action by:

   a. Motion

   or b. Courts initiative

3. Any claim against a party may be severed and proceeded with separately (see Rule 42).

# RULE 18: Joinder of Claims & Remedies

**(a) Joinder of Claims** - A party may join *as many* independent or
   alternate claims as it has against an **opposing** parties. These
   include:
> 1. Original claims
> 2. Counterclaims
> 3. Cross-claims
> 4. third party claims

**(b) Joinder of Remedies** -  Whenever a claim is dependent on the
   outcome of a claim in another action, the two actions may be joined
   into a single action.

# RULE 42: Separate Trials; Consolidation

**(a) Consolidation of Cases** - If cases involve a <u>common question of law
   or fact</u>, a court may:
> 1. Order:
>> a. A joint hearing or trial of any issue in the action
>> or b. A complete consolidation of the actions
> and 2. May make orders regarding the proceedings to avoid
>    costs/delay

**(b) Separate Trials** - A court may split any claims for any of the
   following reasons:
> 1. To avoid prejudice
> 2. To further convenience
> 3. To increase economic efficiency

## B. INTERVENTION

---

### OVERVIEW ——————————————————

- When a party wants to join an action, he should make a Rule 24 **Motion for Intervention**.

- A party seeking to intervene must prove that he has a "*significantly protectable interest*" in the action in order to have a RIGHT to intervene (otherwise intervention is in the court's discretion).

- Requirements for establishing a "*significantly protectable interest*":
    - The person demonstrates a legal interest in the action to intervene as of *right*
    - The right requires a direct, substantial legally protectable interest in the proceedings.
    - The person need not show that he has a legal or equitable interest in jeopardy, but must show it had a "protectable interest" in the litigation's outcome.
    - There must be a direct affect to a *legally cognizable* interest (as opposed to contingent or remote).
    - It requires consideration of all the competing and relevant interests raised by an Application for Intervention.
    - The person's rights and duties are affected by the legislature's disposition.
    - The court may consider any significant *legal effect* of an applicant's interests. A court is not limited to consequences of a strictly legal nature.

- Amicus Curie Briefs - are briefs of non-parties in a pending suit

---

- Often non-parties with an indirect interest in the suit (i.e. they'll be affected by the precedent of the case at bar) write Amicus Curie briefs to the court (instead of participating in action) (ex: Bank X may write an Amicus Curie brief in a suit, between Bank A and B, involving a ruling on the effects of the FDIC on banks, in a suit)
  - Courts often look for outside opinions (ex: lobby groups, Federal agencies, etc.)
  - Request to file Amicus Curie Briefs must be granted before the brief can be filed

- Sometimes non-parties want to become parties instead because they have a much greater interest in the outcome of the suit (i.e. the suit will directly effect them, rather than, where the outcome or law, of the case)

RELEVANT RULES: RULE 24

# RULE 24: Intervention

## (a) Intervention of Right
    i. Anyone may intervene (upon <u>timely</u> application) in an action when:
        (1) A U.S. Statute allows
      or (2) The Applicant claims a *direct* interest in a <u>*related*</u>
          <u>*property/transaction*</u> subject to adjudication, <u>but only if:</u>
          a. The Applicant's interest isn't already properly
            represented in the case.
         or b. The Applicant has a direct "<u>*significantly*</u>
           <u>*protectable*</u>" interest at stake
       and c. Non-intervention will impair/impede the applicant's
          ability to protect that interest
    ii. A party may not intervene if <u>Complete Diversity</u> will not be
      maintained.

## (b) Permissive Intervention
    i. Intervention will be permitted if:
        (1) A U.S. Statute allows
      or (2) The Applicant's claim is related to the <u>main action</u> by
          question of law or fact.
    ii. The court has discretion, and should weigh any <u>delays &</u>
      <u>prejudices</u> to the original parties (resulting from the intervention).

## (c) Procedure - *Motion to Intervene:*
    1. The Intervening party shall serve a <u>*Motion to Intervene*</u> (as per Rule
      5).
    2. <u>Requirements of Motion to Intervene</u> - the motion must:
      a. State the grounds for intervention
   and b. Be accompanied by a pleading describing the claim or
      defense for which intervention is sought.
    3. The same procedure shall be followed when a U.S. statute
      provides for a right to intervene.
    4. If an action involves the constitutionality of an act of Congress,
      the Court shall notify the U.S. Attorney General (if a U.S.
      officer/agent is not already a party).
    5. If an action involves the constitutionality of a State law, the
      Court shall notify the State Attorney General (if a state
      officer/agent is not already a party).

# C. INTERPLEADER

---

## OVERVIEW

- Interpleader is an action between <u>Stakeholders</u> and
  <u>Claimants</u> (Not π's and Defendants).
- Interpleader allows joinder of related claims in <u>one</u>
  action, to avoid inconsistent judgments.
- Interpleader usually involves "replevin," where
  claimants all want a particular piece of property,
  which the stakeholder has.
- Note: The Stakeholder can also be a claimant (and a
  Defendant in a previous action, who brings this action as a stakeholder-
  claimant)
- <u>Forum Shopping</u> - Sometimes interpleader is unfair,
  because it changes the forum that the original πs
  chose.
- As an alternative remedy, courts may enjoin parties,
  forbidding them to receive anything greater than
  what was *originally* at stake (so not to have inconsistent
  verdicts). The enforcement of the judgment will go to
  the court where the interpleader would have been
  held.
- Complete Diversity is <u>Not</u> needed between parties of
  an interpleader from different states (only Minimal
  Diversity, i.e. so its okay if the stakeholder and claimants are from the
  same state, so long as 1 person in the action is diverse).
- There is no need for claims to be "reduced to
  judgment" before a third party may be impleaded.

---

RELEVANT RULES: RULE 22
28 U.S.C. §1335, §1397

# RULE 22: Interpleader

("Rule Interpleader" - requires Complete Diversity)

(1) Interpleader is required if the $\pi$ might be exposed to double liability.
   
    a. Interpleader may take place, even though:

        1. There is no common origin of causes

      or 2. The actions are not identical - but are adverse & independent actions

    b. Defendant may also interplead if he might be held to double liability.

(2) This remedy does not supersede 28 USC §1335, §1397, or §2361.

# §1335: Interpleader

("Statutory Interpleader" - minimal diversity allowed)

(a) The district court has original jurisdiction over a civil action of interpleader if:

    (1) Subject Matter Jurisdiction exists:

        a. The controversy is *greater than or equal to* $500

      and b. **Minimal Diversity**: At least 2 parties need diversity of citizenship (not all)

  and (2) "Stakeholder" posts a bond (or deposits the property in the court)

(b) Interpleader may take place, although

    1. There is no common origin among the titles or claims of the conflicting claimants

  or 2. The actions are not identical, but are adverse and independent actions.

# §1397: Interpleader Venue

A §1335 interpleader action may be brought in a judicial district where *greater than or equal to* 1 claimant resides.

# *XII. JURY*

## *A. RIGHT TO JURY TRIAL*

---

### *OVERVIEW*

- A Party has a right to a jury trial in cases in **law** (not **Equity**) which is protected by the 7th Amendment of the Constitution.
- When **law** and **equity** cases are combined in one action, the court must decide whether or not *each issue* should go to a jury. Any issue that is "legal" in nature should go to the jury.
- The court decision is based on:
    - The <u>custom</u> of ruling the issue in question (whether it has been in law or equity)
    - The <u>remedy</u> sought (money or injunction)
    - The <u>practical abilities</u> and limitations of juries (not considered as much)
- The court should err on the side of allowing a jury trial.
- <u>Waiving Right to a Jury</u>
    - A party will waive its right to a jury if it fails to make a timely demand (<u>10 days</u> from service of pleading)
    - A court may order a jury trial by *Motion, or its own initiative* if a demand is not made.
    - <u>Waiver by contract may be effective if</u>:
        - It is *knowingly* and *intentionally* waived
        - The Party seeking waiver must prove that the contract was both <u>voluntary</u> and <u>informed</u>.
        - <u>Courts look at</u>:
            - Length of the contract
            - Bargaining power between the parties
            - Past business relationships
            - Probability that parties understood the waiver of their right to a jury.

---

---
RELEVANT RULES: RULE 38, RULE 39
---

# RULE 38: Right to a Jury Trial

**(a) Preserved Right** - The rights of a jury trial guaranteed by the 7th Amendment of the Constitution shall be preserved to parties "*inviolate*."

**(b) Demand** - Any party may demand a jury trial on any issue protected by the Constitution or a U.S. statute, by:
> (1) Serving a written "demand" on other parties
> and (2) Filing the demand (pursuant to Rule 5) no later than <u>10 Days</u> from service of the last pleading directed to such issue.

**(c) Specification of Issues**:
> 1. In the demand, the party may specify which issues it wants to be tried by a jury. Otherwise, trial by jury is assumed to be demanded for all issues.
> 2. If a party specifies only some issues, then the other party has <u>10 days</u> (unless the court shortens) to serve a "demand" for other issues he wishes to be tried by a jury.

**(d) Waiver**
> 1. Failure to serve and file (pursuant to this rule) constitutes a waiver of the right to a jury.
> 2. Once a demand is made, it may only be withdrawn if <u>both parties consent</u>.

**(e) Admiralty Claims** - These rules do not apply.

# RULE 39: Trial by Jury or Court

**(a) By Jury** - When a jury trial is demanded, the trial shall proceed as a jury action *unless:*

      (1) The parties both consent on record (either in writing or on oral record in a hearing).

    or (2) Upon motion or the court's own initiative, the court finds that a right to a jury trial on all or some of the issues does not exist under the Constitution or any U.S. statute (ex: the issue arises out of equity).

**(b) By Court**

    1. If no jury demand is made, the court shall try the case.

    2. If a party neglects to make a "demand," the court (upon motion) has *discretion* to allow a jury trial, if it finds that such a demand might have been made *as of right.*

**(c) Advisory Jury and Trial By Consent**

    1. For actions not triable as of right by jury, the court may try an issue with an *advisory jury* (by motion or on its own initiative).

    2. In actions against the U.S. in which a statute provides for trial *without* a jury, a court may only use a jury if both parties agree.

## B. VERDICTS

---

### OVERVIEW

- <u>General Verdict</u> - A "Yes" or "No" decision, without a for the jury's conclusion
- <u>Special Verdicts</u> - often used along with **special interrogatories** to track the jury's thought pattern (making it easier to determine the verdict's validity)
  - Judges retain broad discretion in determining whether or not to use special verdicts/interrogatories.

---

RELEVANT RULES: RULE 51, RULE 49

# RULE 51: Instructions to Jury

1. At the close of evidence (or at such earlier time as the court allows) **any** party may file a written request for the court to instruct the jury on a certain law.
2. Prior to their arguments to the jury, the court shall inform counsel of its proposed action based on their requests.
3. The court may instruct the jury before or after the arguments, or both.
4. Objections to giving or failure to give jury instructions must be made *before* the jury retires to consider its verdict.
5. Objections must specifically state the grounds for objection.

# RULE 49: Special Verdicts and Interrogatories

**(a) Special Verdicts** - The court may require a jury to return only a **special verdict.**

    1. The special verdict must be in the form of a special <u>written</u> finding upon each issue of fact.

    2. The court may submit to the jury:

        a. Written questions susceptible of absolute or other brief answers

    or b. Written forms of the several special findings which could properly be made from the evidence or pleadings

    or c. Other methods of submitting issues (as it deems appropriate)

    3. The court shall give the jury instructions as necessary to facilitate a jury decision.

    4. If the court omits any issue of fact for the jury to decide, the parties must demand submission *before the jury retires*.

    5. The court may decide those issues omitted.

**(b) General Verdict**

    1. The court may submit forms for a **general verdict** accompanied by *written* interrogatories on issues of fact necessary to decide a general verdict.

    2. The court shall give appropriate instructions to help the jurors make their decision.

    3. When the general verdict and written answers are *"harmonious,"* appropriate judgment shall be made.

    4. <u>Inconsistencies:</u>

        a. <u>When answers are consistent with each other, yet 1 or more answer is inconsistent with the general verdict,</u> the judge may:

            1. Affirm jury's verdict

          or 2. Enter judgment in accordance with their answers (and not the general verdict).

          or 3. Send the jury back for further considerations

          or 4. Order a new trial

        b. <u>When answers are inconsistent with each other and inconsistent with the general verdict,</u> the judge shall:

            1. Send the jury back for further considerations

          or 2. Order a new trial

# XII. JUDGMENT

## A. JUDGMENT AS A MATTER OF LAW: ("JNOV")

---

### OVERVIEW ─────────────────────

- A "JNOV" (judgment as a matter of law) motion may only be considered <u>after</u> the jury has submitted its verdict.
- In considering a JNOV motion, the court must weigh all the evidence in the light (and with all reasonable inference), *most favorable* to the party opposed to the motion.
- <u>Tests</u>:
    - JNOV may be granted if:
        - Reasonable people could <u>not</u> have arrived at the jury's verdict
        - or • There is no *legally sufficient* evidentiary basis for a reasonable jury to find for the non-moving party
    - JNOV may be denied if evidence shows that reasonable people *might* have reached the same conclusion as the jury did.
    - Courts may also look to see if:
        - The jury was properly instructed
        - The evidence is sufficient enough to support the movant's position
        - Special Interrogatories, if any, contain proper standards of liability

---

RELEVANT RULES: RULE 50

# RULE 50: Judgments and Jury Trials:

**(a) Judgment as a Matter of Law** (JNOV; "Directed Verdict")

    (1) The court may grant a motion for judgment as a matter of law, if, after being heard, there is no *legally sufficient evidentiary basis* for a *reasonable* jury to have found for a party on a certain issue (because it would be contrary to controlling law).

    (2) Requirements for a Motion for Judgment as a Matter of Law

        a. Must be made _before_ the case is submitted to the jury

        b. Must specify the judgment sought

        c. Must state the applicable rule of law and its relationship to the facts

        d. Must be made _after_ the non-movant has been <u>fully heard</u>

**(b) Renewal for Judgment After Trial; Alternative Motion for New Trial**

    1. <u>Renewal of Motion for Judgment after Trial</u>:

        a. If the original motion is denied, the court is deemed to have submitted the case to the jury.

        b. A jury verdict will be subject to a later determination of the legal questions raised by the motion.

        c. The motion may be "renewed" after the verdict by filing and serving it within <u>10 days</u> after *entry of judgment.*

    2. <u>Alternative Motion for a New Trial</u> -  May be requested in the *alternative* or *joined* with renewal of the motion (See Rule 50(c)).

    3. <u>Judgment on the Renewed Motion</u>

        a. _If a Verdict is returned_, the court may:

            1. Allow the original judgment to stand

        or 2. Direct entry of judgment as a matter of law (reverse)

        or  3. Order a new trial

        b. _If No Verdict Returned_, the court may:

            1. Direct entry of judgment as a matter of law

        or 2. Order a new trial

## (c) Conditions of Granting Judgment as a Matter of Law

(1) If a motion for judgment is granted, the court must also rule on a <u>motion for a new trial</u> (if it was made) as follows:

- The Court must decide whether a new trial should be granted if the judgment is vacated or reversed after the JNOV
- The court must describe specific grounds for granting or denying the motion for retrial.
- Even if the motion for a new trial is conditionally granted (i.e. if the JNOV is later vacated or reversed), the judgment is still final. If the JNOV is later reversed on appeal, the new trial goes forward (unless the appellate court ordered otherwise).
- If the motion for retrial is denied, the denial may be appealed. If the JNOV is later reversed on appeal, the appellate court determines what subsequent proceedings take place.

(2) If judgment as a matter of law has been rendered against a party, that party may serve a motion for a new trial (under Rule 59) no later than <u>10 days</u> after the judgment was entered.

## (d) Denial of a Motion for Judgment as a Matter of Law

1. The successful party may, on appeal, request a new trial, if: the motion was *denied*, and the appellate court finds that the <u>trial court erred</u> in denying the motion for judgment.
2. If the <u>appellate court reverses</u> the trial court's judgment it may also find that:
   a. The appellee is entitled to a new trial
   or b. The trial court shall determine if a new trial should be granted

# B. NEW TRIALS

---

## OVERVIEW ——————————————————

- The granting of a new trial is in the court's discretion.
- **Factors Considered**:
  - Was the Verdict Excessive? What was the *maximum amount* supported by the evidence?
  - Were excessive damages caused by "Passion or Prejudice?" Can that be proven?
- Choosing between New Trial and JNOV
  - New Trial - "Passion and Prejudice" – against the *clear weight of evidence*
  - JNOV – impossible for a *reasonable* jury to decide
- New Trial and Remittitur
  - When a party is entitled to a new trial, he has the option of accepting a **remittitur** – a reduction in judgment – instead.
  - Courts will usually prefer a remittitur:
    - Remittitur - can be used for verdicts that give *too much* recovery.
    - New Trial - can be used when issues were affected by *"passion or prejudice."*
  - If a party refuses remittitur and damages issues are clearly independent of liability issues, a new trial (if granted) may be limited to the question of damages.
  - If a court decides to use a remittitur, it must first offer the party a choice between:
    - Accepting a reduction in damages
    - or • Proceeding with a new trial
  - If remittitur is chosen, the court may not reduce damages below the *"maximum amount supported by the evidence"*
  - Such *maximum award* should be reasonably proportioned to the amount of actual damages.

---

RELEVANT RULES: RULE 58, RULE 59, RULE 52

# RULE 58: Entry Of Judgment

(1) The clerk shall prepare, sign, and enter judgment (without waiting for the court's direction to do so), in the following situations:
>    a. The Court's Decision, if:
>>        1. The decision was made without a jury
>>    and 2. The decision *either:*
>>>            i. Denies relief
>>>        or ii. Awards a "sum certain"
>    or b. The General Verdict

(2) The Judge must first approve the clerk's form if judgment is entered upon:
>>        a. The court's decision (non-jury)
>>    or b. A special verdict
>>    or c. A general verdict with special interrogatories

3. Each judgment is be recorded on a separate document.

4. There must be no delays in entering orders to tax costs or award fees.

5. Attorneys may provide the form of judgment, which would be filed with the Clerk upon the judge's approval.

6. Judgment entry must be done pursuant to Rule 79(a).

# RULE 59: New Trials and Judgment Amendments

**(a) Grounds** - A new trial may be granted on all or some of the issues in the following instances:

(1) <u>Trial By Jury</u> - allowed for any reason courts have (until now) allowed a new trial (See Rule 60(b)).

(2) <u>Trial Without a Jury</u> –

    a. Allowed for any reason the courts have (until now) allowed a rehearing.

    b. Upon motion for new trial, courts may:

        1. Open judgment (if one has been entered)

      or 2. Take additional testimony

      or 3. Amend a finding of fact

      or 4. Amend a finding/ conclusions of law

      or 5. Make new findings of fact or law

      or 6. Direct entry of a new judgment (or affirm the original judgment)

**(b) Time Limitation** - The motion must be served no later than <u>10 Days</u> after entry of judgment.

**(c) Serving Affidavits**

1. When a motion for a new trial is based on affidavits, the affidavits shall be served <u>with the motion</u>.

2. The opposing party has <u>10 Days</u> after service of the motion to serve opposing affidavits (may be extended to no more than <u>20 days</u> (total) if good cause is shown or the parties agree).

**(d) New Trial on Court's Initiative**

1. The court may order a new trial on its own initiative, for any reason it may have granted a new trial by motion.

2. The court may order a new trial for reasons not specified in the motion *after* giving <u>notice</u> and an <u>opportunity</u> to be heard.

3. The court must specify the grounds for its decision

4. The court must order a new trial no later than <u>10 days</u> after entry of judgment.

**(e) Motion to Alter or Amend Judgment** - Must be served no later than <u>10 Days</u> after entry of judgment.

# RULE 52: Findings By The Court

## (a) Effect

1. <u>Scope</u>: This rule applies to actions tried <u>without a jury</u> or <u>with an advisory jury</u>.
2. The court shall state *separately* its conclusions of law and its findings of fact.
3. Judgment shall be entered pursuant to Rule 58.
4. In granting or refusing interlocutory injunctions, the court must also specifically state findings of facts and law as grounds for its conclusion.
5. <u>Review of Facts</u> (on appeal); <u>Standard of Review</u>:
   a. The findings of fact shall only be set aside if they are *clearly erroneous*.
   b. *Due regard* must be given to the trial judge's opportunity to determine a witnesses' credibility.
6. Findings of a master shall be considered findings of the court.
7. Findings of fact may be stated orally (and recorded) or written in an opinion or memorandum.
8. Findings of fact and conclusions of law are not needed for motions under Rule 12 or Rule 56.

## (b) Amendment

1. <u>Motion to Amend</u>:
   a. A motion for amendment may be made within <u>10 Days</u> after entry of judgment.
   b. The motion may be made along with a motion for a new trial (pursuant to Rule 59).
2. The court may amend its findings or make additional findings, and change the judgment accordingly.
3. When the court makes findings of fact, a party may raise a question of <u>sufficiency of the evidence</u>, *without:*
   a. Making a motion to amend
   b. Making a motion for judgment
   c. Raising objections to such findings in the district court

**(c) Judgment on Partial Findings** ("Mini-trial" or "Partial Judgment")

    1. <u>Scope</u>: This subsection applies to trials heard <u>without a jury</u>.

    2. A judge may enter judgment as a matter of law *before* all the evidence is heard if:

        a. A party has been <u>fully heard</u> on certain issues

        and b. The claim or defense is controlled by the issues

        and c. The only way the case could be won is if one particular issue was found in favor of that party

        and d. The court did not find the issue in favor of that party

    3. The court may also wait until the close of all the evidence to make its decision.

    4. The court shall support its decision as required by Rule 52(a).

## C. RELIEF FROM JUDGMENT

RELEVANT RULES: RULE 60

# RULE 60: Relief From Judgment

**(a)** For **clerical mistakes** (and mistakes arising out of <u>oversight</u> or
<u>omission</u>) in judgments, orders, or other parts of the record:
>    1. Such errors may be corrected by motion or on the court's
>        initiative
>    2. While an appeal is pending, the errors may be corrected
>        before the appeal is docketed
>    3. Once the appeal is pending, leave of the appellate court is
>        needed for a correction to be made.

**(b) Relief from Judgment**
>    i. The court may relieve a party (or its legal representative) from a final
>        judgment, order, or proceeding if:
>> (1) There was mistake, inadvertence, surprise, or excusable
>>     neglect.
>> or (2) Newly discovered evidence was found, which by *due
>>     diligence* could not have been discovered in time to move
>>     for a new trial.
>> or (3) There was fraud, misrepresentation, or other misconduct
>>     on the part of an adverse party
>> or (4) The judgment is void (ex: jurisdiction is not appropriate).
>> or (5) *Either:*
>>> a. The judgment was satisfied
>>> or b. The judgment has been released or discharged
>>> or c. A prior judgment, upon which the judgment is based,
>>>     is reversed
>>> or d. It is no longer equitable that the judgment should have
>>>     prospective application
>> or (6) There exists any other reason justifying relief from the
>>     operation of the judgment.

ii. <u>Time to Make Motion</u>
    1. "<u>Term Rule</u>": For reasons (1), (2), and (3), a motion must be made within <u>1 year</u> from when the judgment or order was entered.
    2. For reasons (4), (5), and (6), a motion must be made within a *<u>reasonable time</u>* from when the judgment was entered or taken.

## D. DISMISSAL OF ACTIONS

# RULE 41: Dismissal Of Actions

**(a) Voluntary Dismissal**:
  (1) <u>By Plaintiff or Stipulation</u>:
      a. An action may be dismissed by the $\pi$ without a court order by:
         (i) filing a notice of dismissal at any time before service of an <u>answer</u> or <u>motion for summary judgment</u> is made (whichever is <u>sooner</u>)
        or (ii) filing a stipulation of dismissal singed by all parties who have appeared in the action
      b. Dismissal shall be <u>without prejudice</u>, unless:
        1. Otherwise stated in the notice
        2. The notice of dismissal operates as an adjudication upon the merits
        3. The case is filed by a $\pi$ who has already dismissed the action for the same claim in another court
      c. This subsection is subject to Rule 23(e), Rule 66, and any other U.S. statute.
  (2) <u>By Order of Court:</u>
      a. Unless dismissed under 41(a)(1), an action shall only be dismissed upon a court order.
      b. If a counterclaim has been pleaded by the Defendant prior to service of the $\pi$'s notice of dismissal then:
        1. The case cannot be dismissed if the counterclaim cannot remain as an independent action.
        2. $\pi$'s claim can be dismissed if the counterclaim can remain as an independent action.
      c. Dismissal of 41(a)(2) actions is <u>without prejudice</u>.

**(b) Involuntary Dismissal:**
    1. Defendant may move for a dismissal of any claim if π:
        a. Fails to prosecute
      or b. Fails to comply with the Federal Rules of Civil Procedure
      or c. Fails to comply with any court order
    2. Dismissal under 41(b) is <u>with prejudice</u>, unless the court:
        a. States otherwise
      or b. Dismissed the case for <u>lack of jurisdiction</u>
      or c. Dismissed the case for <u>improper venue</u>
      or d. Dismissed the case for <u>failure to join a party</u> (pursuant to Rule 19)

**(c) Dismissal of Counterclaims**
    1. This rule applies to any claims, including:
        a. Counterclaims
      and b. Cross-claims
      and c. Third party claims
    2. If the claimant alone makes a voluntary dismissal (pursuant to 41(a)(1)), it must be made:
        a. Before responsive pleadings are served
        b. Before introduction of evidence (at trial or hearing), if there are no responsive pleadings

**(d) Costs of Previously Dismissed Actions** - If π previously dismissed an action and is now reinstating it (i.e. bringing an action based on or including the <u>same</u> claim against the <u>same</u> Defendant), the court may impose costs for the previously dismissed action.

# *XIII. APPEALS*

## *OVERVIEW*

**Interlocutory Appeals** (28 USC §1292):
- §1291 gives the Appellate Courts jurisdiction over all "final judgments" of a District Court, i.e. ordinarily in Federal Courts, a District Court decision cannot be appealed until the entire case has been adjudicated (i.e. there is a final judgment).
- Exception: When an *immediate* appeal is needed to prevent further, perhaps unnecessary, litigation (ex: a decision on jurisdiction), an "interlocutory" appeal may be granted.
- Factors Weighed in Determining Whether or Not to Accept an Interlocutory Appeal:
    - If the decision would *conclusively* determine the disputed question
    - If it resolves an important and *independent* issue (ex: whether Personal Jurisdiction exists)
    - If the issue is effectively *unreviewable* on appeal after final judgment
    - Courts should not look at the burden on the Defendant to later prove that there was an erroneous trial.
    - §1292 – Gives the Court of Appeals the power to review Special Interlocutory Decisions:
        - **Court of Appeals has the power** to hear matters before final judgment occurs when the decision deals with:
            - Injunctions- Interlocutory orders granting, continuing, modifying, refusing, or dissolving injunctions
            - Receivers – Interlocutory Orders appointing receivers
            - Admiralty Cases
        - **Subject Matter Jurisdiction:**
            - The court has *discretion* to hear all other pre-final-judgment decisions

RELEVANT RULES: 28 U.S.C. §1291, §1292

# §1291: Appellate Jurisdiction

The **appellate court** has jurisdiction of appeals from all final decisions of the district courts.

# §1292: Interlocutory Decisions

**(a)** The **appellate court** has the power to hear a case before final judgment when:
  (1) Injunctions- There is an interlocutory order granting, continuing, modifying, refusing, or dissolving an injunction
  (2) Receivers - There is an interlocutory order appointing a receiver (within the meaning of Rule 9)
  (3) Admiralty cases

**(b) Judge's Request to Appeal**
  1. If not included in (a), a district judge may request an interlocutory order appeal by writing to the appellate court within 10 days after her order, if she believes there is a controlling question of law where there is substantial ground for difference of opinion, and an appeal may *materially advance* the ultimate termination of the case.
  2. The appellate court has discretion to accept such a request.

**(c)** U.S. appellate courts have **exclusive jurisdiction** of:
  (1) Any case covered by §1295
  and (2) Patent infringement cases which are final, except for an accounting (Where jurisdiction would otherwise lie in the Court of Appeals for the Federal Circuit)

**(d) Specific Issues:**
- i. The appellate court has discretion to take a case if:
    - 1. The application for appeal is made within <u>10 days</u> of an order is entered
- and 2. *Either:*
    - a. The Chief Judge of the Court of International Trade issues a 256(b) interlocutory order.
    - or b. The Chief Judge of the Court of Federal Claims issues a 798(b) interlocutory order.
    - or c. Any judge of the Court of International Trade/Court of Federal Claims issues an interlocutory order.
- and 3. There is a *substantial ground* for difference of opinion on a controlling question of law.
- and 4. An immediate appeal may *materially advance* the termination of the suit.
- ii. <u>Applicability</u>
    - (1) The above rules apply to the <u>Court of International Trade</u>.
    - (2) The above rules apply to the <u>Court of Federal Claims</u>.
    - (3) Proceedings <u>shall not</u> stay unless the district court or appellate court so orders.
    - (4) <u>Motion To Transfer</u>
        - (A) The appellate court has exclusive jurisdiction over all of the district court's <u>ordering</u>, <u>granting</u>, or <u>denying</u> of motions to transfer a case (pursuant to 28 USC §1631).
        - (B) Actions <u>must</u> be stayed (put on hold) until <u>60 days</u> after the court has ruled upon a motion to transfer to the Court of Federal Claims. The time may be extended until after the appeal is decided (if an appeal is taken).

# E-Z RULES

## FOR THE

# FEDERAL RULES

## OF

# CIVIL PROCEDURE

# and Selected Statutes

# TABLE OF CONTENTS

## FOR

# THE FEDERAL RULES
## OF
# CIVIL PROCEDURE

### AND
### *SELECTED STATUTES*

# TABLE OF CONTENTS

### FOR

# THE FEDERAL RULES
### OF
# CIVIL PROCEDURE

### AND
### *SELECTED STATUTES*

## I. SCOPE OF RULES

## II. COMMENCEMENT OF ACTION; SERVICE OF PROCESS, PLEADINGS, MOTIONS AND ORDERS

## III. PLEADINGS AND MOTIONS

# IV. PARTIES

# V. DISCOVERY AND DEPOSITIONS

# VI. TRIALS

# VII. JURY AND TRIAL RULES

# VIII. JUDGMENT

# IX. SPECIAL PROCEEDINGS

# X. DISTRICT COURTS AND CLERKS

# XI. GENERAL PROVISIONS

## SELECTED STATUTES

## INTERPLEADER STATUTES

# VENUE STATUTES

# REMOVAL STATUTES

# APPENDIX

*Discovery Rules*

# *I. SCOPE OF RULES*

## RULE 1: Scope of Rules

    a. <u>Applicability:</u> These rules govern the procedure for all civil cases in the U.S. District Courts, including suits in law, equity, and admiralty (with the exceptions stated in Rule 81).

    b. <u>Objective:</u> *"To secure the just, speedy, and inexpensive determination of every action"* (i.e. There is no distinction between law and equity)

## RULE 2: One Form of Action

"There shall be one form of action to be known as *civil action*."

# II. COMMENCEMENT OF ACTION; SERVICE OF PROCESS, PLEADINGS, MOTIONS AND ORDERS

## RULE 3: Commencement of Action

"A civil action is commenced by filing a complaint with the court."


## RULE 4: Summons

**(a) Summons Form:**
>    1. <u>Requirements</u> - The Summons must:
>        a. Be directed to the Defendant
>        b. Be signed by the clerk
>        c. Bear the seal of the court
>        d. Identify the name of court
>        e. Identify the names of the parties
>        f. State the name and address of the π's attorney (or π, if not represented).
>        g. Specify the time for the Defendant to appear to defend himself (before a default occurs).
>        h. Notify the Defendant that the consequence for failing to appear would be <u>default judgment</u> in favor of π.
>    2. The court may allow a summons to be amended.

**(b) Issuing the Summons:**
>    1. After the π files the complaint, he may present the summons to the clerk for a signature and seal.
>    2. If the summons is in proper form, the clerk must sign, seal, and issue it to the π for service on the Defendant.
>    3. The clerk will issue as many summonses as there are Ds.
>    4. π or π's attorney is responsible for delivering the Summons and Complaint to Defendant.

**(c) Service:**
  (1) Plaintiff's Obligations:
      1. A Summons shall be served together with a copy of the complaint.
      2. π is responsible for service (see Rule 4(m) for time limits).
      3. π must furnish the process server with the necessary copies of the summons and complaint.

  (2) Summons and Complaint
      A. Qualifications to Serve:
          (i) Anyone *at least* 18 years old
        and (ii) A Non-Party to the suit
      B. U.S. Marshall to Serve:
          i. π *may* request a U.S. Marshall or a specially Appointed agent to serve.
          ii. π *must* request a U.S. Marshall or a Specially appointed agent to serve if the π is proceeding in *forma pauperis* (pursuant to 28 USC §1915)or as a seaman.

**(d) Waiver of Service:**

  (1) A Defendant who waives service does not waive any objection to *venue* or *jurisdiction* of the court.

  (2) Sending a Waiver of Service Notice:
      i. To avoid costs, the π may notify the Defendant of the action with a *"Waiver of Service Notice"* and request that the Defendant waive service of the summons.

      ii. Any Defendant who has received a proper Waiver of Service Notice has a duty to avoid unnecessary costs of serving the summons.

      iii. If the Defendant refuses to waive good cause, the Defendant must pay the costs of service.

iv. <u>Requirements for Waiver of Service Notice</u>:

(A) **In Writing**:
1. <u>Individuals</u>: Notice must be addressed directly to the Defendant.
2. <u>Corporations/Associations</u>: Notice must be addressed to either an officer, managing/general agent, or agent appointed by law.

(B) **First Class Mail** - π must send the notice by first class mail or other reliable means.

(C) **Copy of Complaint:** The notice must:
1. include a copy of the **Complaint**
and 2. identify the **forum** (the court) in which the complaint has been filed.

(D) **Consequences** - π must specify the consequences of compliance and of failure to comply with request (see official forms)

(E) **Dated** - The date when the waiver request was sent must specified.

(F) **Time Limit**
1. π must inform the Defendant of the time limit by which the Defendant must notify π of his intention to waive service.
2. The time limit must be at least <u>30 days</u> from the *date sent* for return (<u>60 days</u> if sent to a foreign country).

(G) **Supplies** - must supply Defendant with:
1. Extra copy of Notice and Request.
2. Prepaid means of return (ex: Self-Addressed Stamped Envelope).

(3) <u>Time for Answer with Waiver:</u> Defendant may wait <u>60 days</u> after the request is sent to furnish an <u>Answer</u> (<u>90 days</u> if sent to a foreign country). Note: Although the Defendant may send an *answer* after 60 days, the response to the notice of waiver **must** still be sent within 30 days.

(4) <u>Commencement of Action With Waiver</u>: The action proceeds as normal (except for the time for filing an Answer) is considered to have started once π has filed the waiver notice with the clerk. No proof of service is needed.

(5) <u>Costs to Defendant for Denying Waiver</u>: The Defendant will be responsible for the following costs if he does not consent to the waiver of notice:

a. Cost subsequently incurred in order to effectuate service and b. Costs of any motion needed to collect service costs, including *reasonable* attorney's fees.

(e) **Service on Individuals**: - If the Defendant does not waive service, π may serve according to:

(1) <u>The State law for service</u> - π may rely on the state law of *either*:

a. The state where the District Court (in which the action is being brought) is located

or b. The state where service is being made

or (2) <u>The federal law for service</u> - π may choose any of the following methods to serve under Federal law:

a. **Personal Service** - π must personally serve to the individual (actual hand delivery).

or b. **Abode Service** - to a resident in Defendant's *usual place of abode* (no business service).

or c. **Substitute Service** - to an authorized agent.

(f) **Service Upon Individuals in a Foreign Country** - Unless waived, service may be made outside of the U.S.:

(1) <u>By any Internationally agreed method</u> if it is *reasonably calculated to give notice* (ex: Hague Convention).

or (2) <u>If no Internationally agreed method of service</u>, then:

(A) Service laws of the foreign country

or (B) As directed by a foreign authority (in response to a letter rogatory/request)

or (C) By (unless prohibited by the foreign country):

(i) **Personal service** - delivery to the individual of the summons and complaint

or (ii) **Mail** - registered mail to be dispatched by the court clerk in Defendant's country.

or (3) <u>As directed by forum court</u> (i.e. in the U.S.) as long as it is not prohibited by an international agreement.

**(g) Service upon Infants/Incompetents** - Use state law (if outside of U.S., refer to 4(f)).

**(h) Service on Corporations/Associations:**
    i. <u>Applicability:</u> This subsection applies
        a. Unless another federal law provides otherwise.
      and b. If the Defendant is *either:*
            1. A Domestic or Foreign Corporation
          or 2. A Partnership
          or 3. An unincorporated association subject to suit under a common name
      and c. A Waiver of Service has not been obtained and filed.
    ii. <u>Service under this subsection shall be effective when:</u>
        (1) State law is followed (as per Rule 4(e)(1))
      or (2) If the Defendant is a Foreign Corporation, and Rule 4(f) was used
      or 3. Delivering a copy to an *<u>authorized</u>* **General Agent**, **Officer**, or **Manager** (and mailing a copy to the Defendant if the statute so requires).

**(i) Service Upon the United States**
    (1) <u>Effective Service</u>
        (a) Delivering to:
            1. The U.S. attorney for the forum district
          or 2. The U.S. attorney's assistant or clerk
          or 3. Registered or Certified mailing to civil process clerk
      and (b) Sending a Registered or Certified mailing to the U.S. Attorney General
      and (c) Delivering a copy to an officer or agency, if a U.S. agency or officer is involved
    (2) <u>To a U.S. Agency</u> - Delivery and Certified Mail to an officer/agency
    (3) *Reasonable time* is allowed for 4(i) service

**(j) Service Upon Foreign, State, or Local Governments:**
   (1) <u>Foreign State, Political Subdivision, etc.:</u> Service is made pursuant to 28 USC §1608.
   (2) <u>U.S./State/Municipal Corporation or Organization</u> *either*:
      a. Serve the <u>CEO</u>
     <u>*or*</u> b. Use state law service

**(k) Territorial Limits of Effective Service**
   (1) Service of a summons or filing of a 4(e) waiver is sufficient to establish **Personal Jurisdiction** if:
      (A) The forum district's state laws allow it.
     or (B) The Defendant is a Joined Party (as per Rule 14 and 19) and is served within <u>100 miles</u> from where the summons was issued
     or (C) The Defendant is subject to the Federal Interpleader jurisdiction (as per 28 USC §1335)
     or (D) It is authorized by a U.S. statute
   (2) Defendant <u>Not Subject to Jurisdiction of Any State:</u> A waiver of service notice or service of a summons is effective to establish personal jurisdiction if:
      a. The Defendant is not subject to the jurisdiction of any state
    and b. The exercise of jurisdiction over the Defendant is consistent with the Constitution and laws of the U.S. (ex: State Minimum Contact is greater than the Constitutional Minimum Contact)
    and c. The claims arise under Federal Law

**(l) Proof of Service** (if service is not waived):
   1. If service is not made by a U.S. Marshal, an <u>affidavit of service</u> is required as proof of service.
   2. <u>Foreign Countries:</u> Proof of service may be attained:
      a. According to treaty agreements (if served pursuant to 4(f)(1))
     or b. With a Registered Mail receipt - if mailed (pursuant to 4(f)(2),(3))
   3. Failure to prove service does not affect validity of service.
   4. A Court may allow proof of service to be amended.

**(m) Time Limit for Service**
   1. Service must be made within <u>120 days</u> after filing the complaint.
   2. If service is not made in time the case will either be:
      a. Automatically dismissed (without prejudice)
   or b. Service will be demanded within a specified time
   3. If π shows *good cause*, the court may extend the time to serve (or the service period).
   4. This subsection does not apply to service to Foreign Persons (Rule 4(f)) or Foreign Corporations (see Rule 4(j)(1)).

**(n) Seizure of Property:**
   (1) <u>Notice</u>
      a. A court may have jurisdiction over property if a U.S. statute so provides.
      b. <u>Notice</u> to claimants of the property to be seized shall be sent, *either*:
         1. As provided by the statute
         2. By service of a summons under this rule
   (2) <u>In-Rem Jurisdiction</u>:
      a. If Personal Jurisdiction (in the district where the action is brought) over Defendant cannot be obtained with *reasonable effort* the court may assert "<u>In-Rem</u>" jurisdiction by seizing the Defendant's assets that are located in the forum district.
      b. The court must seize property according to the State law (in which the forum district court is located).

# RULE 5: Service and Filing of Pleadings and Papers

**(a) Service: When Required**
1. Service is required for:
   a. Every order which is required, by its terms, to be served
   b. Every pleading made after the initial complaint (*unless* the court orders otherwise because there are many Defendants)
   c. Every paper relating to discovery
   d. Every written motion (*unless* it's being heard *ex parte*)
   e. Every written notice
   f. Every demand
   g. Every appearance
   h. Every offer of judgment
   i. Every designation of record on appeal
   j. Any *"similar papers"*
2. Service is not required to parties in default (because they failed to appear) *unless* the π wants to assert a new or additional claim of relief to the defaulting Defendant.
3. Seizure Actions: In actions begun by seizing property, where no person is named as a Defendant, any service required to be made prior to the filing of the answer, claim or appearance must be made to the person in custody or possession of the property at the time of seizure.

**(b) Serving Papers**
1. Whenever rules *require* or *permit* service to a party's attorney, service shall be made to the attorney (unless the court specifically orders service to the individual party).
2. Method of Serving an Attorney:
   a. "Delivering" to attorney (see below)
   or b. Mailing to the attorney/party at last known address
   or c. Leaving it with the clerk if no address is known
3. Valid "Delivery" includes:
   a. Handing it to an attorney or party
   b. Leaving papers at the attorney/party's office with a clerk (or someone in charge)
   c. Leaving papers in a conspicuous place in the attorney/party's office (if no one is in charge)
   d. Leaving in attorney/party's usual place of abode with a **resident** (of suitable age) if:

1. The Party/attorney has no office
2. The Party/attorney's office is closed

e. *Service by mail is complete upon mailing*.

### (c) Serving Numerous Defendants

1. A Court may (upon motion or the court's own initiative) exempt a Defendant from service of pleadings/replies to other Defendants.
2. Consequences of the Court's Decision: If the court exempts a Defendant from serving other Defendants:
   a. The other Defendants will be deemed to have denied or avoided any:
      1. Counterclaims
      or 2. Cross-claims
      or 3. Affirmative defenses
   and b. The filing of the pleadings and service on the $\pi$ is considered sufficient notice to all other Defendants in the case
3. A copy of every such order shall be served upon the parties as the court directs.

### (d) Filing

1. All papers to be served after the complaint must be filed with the court along with a certificate of service.
2. Such a filing must be done within a reasonable time after service.
3. A Court may (upon motion or its own initiative) exempt discovery materials from this filing requirement.

### (e) Method of Filing[1]

1. Filing is normally be made by filing papers with the clerk of the court.
2. The judge may permit the papers to be filed directly with the judge (the judge will then indicate the filing date and give the papers to the clerk).
3. A Clerk may not refuse to file any paper solely because it is not presented in its proper form.
4. Faxed papers may be used if local rules permit.

---

[1] This rule was amended in 1996 to permit electronic filing in district courts under certain circumstances. The amendment permits federal courts to establish local rules to allow documents to be filed, signed or verified by electronic means, provided those means are consistent with technical standards (if any) established by the Judicial Conference of the United States.

# RULE 6: Time

**(a) Computation**
    1. Computation of any time requirements under these rules:
        a. The period begins the day *after* the act, default, or event occurs.
        b. The last day of the period is be included in the computation, *unless*:
            1. The last day is a weekend or legal holiday
        or 2. The time limitation for filing is extended to the first day the office of the clerk is open if:
            a. The office of the clerk is closed
          or b. The office of the clerk is inaccessible due to weather conditions
    2. For periods <u>less than 11 days</u>, weekends and legal holidays are not included in computation.

**(b) Enlargement**
    i. A Court may use its discretion to extend time periods:
        (1) <u>With or without a motion</u> - if a request is made before the expiration of the original time period.
        (2) <u>Upon motion</u> - after expiration of original time period, if the failure to act was caused by "*<u>excusable neglect</u>*."
    ii. A Court is limited in extending time periods to the extent provided in the following rules:
        a. 50(b)
        b. 50(c)(2)
        c. 52(b)
        d. 59(b)
        e. 59(d)
        f. 59(e)
        g. 60(b)

**(c) Rescinded**

**(d) Time Period for Motions**
 1. Written motions and notices of hearing may be served no later than <u>5 days</u> before the date specified for hearing, <u>*unless*</u>:
  a. A different time period is specified in the FRCP
  b. The motion may be heard *ex parte*
 2. Affidavits supporting a motion shall be served with the motion (except as otherwise provided by 59(c)).
 3. Opposing affidavits may be served no later than <u>1 Day</u> before the hearing (unless permitted by the court).

**(e) Service By Mail** - Whenever service is properly done by mail, <u>3 days</u> will be *added* to the time limitation (for any subsequent acts or proceedings).

# *III. PLEADINGS AND MOTIONS*

## RULE 7:  Pleadings Allowed

**(a) Pleadings:**
>  Allowable pleadings include:
>>  1. The Complaint
>>  2. The Answer
>>  3. A Reply to a Counterclaim
>>  4. An Answer to a Cross-claim
>>  5. A third party complaint (if that party was not an original party under Rule 14)
>>  6. A third party answer (if a third party complaint was served)
>>  7. A Reply to an answer or third party answer (allowed only upon court orders)

**(b) Motions and Other Papers**
>  (1) Requirements for an Application for an Order:
>>  a. Must be made in writing:
>>>  1. Writing requirement will be fulfilled if the motion is stated in a written notice of the hearing of the motion.
>>>  2. Writing requirement is not necessary if a motion is made at a hearing or trial.
>>  b. Shall state grounds for motions with "*particularity*"
>>  c. Shall state relief sought
>  (2) All rules regarding form of pleadings and captioning (numbering) of rules apply.
>  (3) All motions must be signed in accordance with Rule 11.

**(c) Demurrers, Pleas, etc., Abolished:**
>  Demurrers, pleas, and exceptions (for insufficiency of a pleading) shall not be used.

# RULE 8:   General Rules of Pleadings

**(a) Claims for Relief** - must contain:
>    (1) A Short plain statement of <u>jurisdiction</u> <small>(unless the court already has it)</small>
>    (2) A Short and plain statement that the <u>Pleader is entitled to relief</u>
>    (3) <u>Relief sought</u> <small>("demand for judgment")</small> -*Alternative types of relief may be demanded*

**(b) Defenses; Form of Denials**
>    1. The Pleader shall state <small>(in plain & short terms)</small> defenses to each claim asserted, and <u>admit</u> or <u>deny</u> the allegations
>    2. If the Pleader is without sufficient knowledge or information <small>(to admit or deny)</small> the Pleader may so state <small>(a.k.a. "D.K.I.")</small>. In such a case, the court will consider it as if the Pleader *denied* the allegations.
>    3. Denials must challenge the substance of the denied allegations.
>    4. If the Pleader intends to deny only a part of an allegation, he shall specify what is true and deny only the remainder.
>    5. <u>Types of Denials which a Pleader may make</u>:
>> a. *Specific denial* - applying to only parts of the pleadings
>> or b. *Complete denial* - applying to entire complaint
>> or c. *General denial* - applying to the entire complaint, except paragraphs specified

**(c) Affirmative Defenses**
>    1. <u>Types of Affirmative Defenses:</u>

| | |
|---|---|
| a. Accord and Satisfaction | k. Estoppel |
| b. Arbitration and Award | l. Failure of Consideration |
| c. Assumption of Risk | m. Fraud |
| d. Contributory Negligence | n. Illegality |
| e. Discharge in Bankruptcy | o. Injury |
| f. Duress | p. Injury by fellow servant |
| g. Laches | q. Payment |
| h. License | r. Release |
| i. Res Judicata | s. Statute of Frauds |
| j. Waiver | t. Any other matter constituting an Avoidance or Affirmative Defense |

    2. If the Pleader makes a mistake and puts Counterclaims as affirmative defenses, the Court may treat it as if it were without mistakes.

### (d) Effect of Failure to Deny

    1. Any denials omitted are deemed to have been admitted, unless:

        a. A responsive pleading was not required

    or b. The omission involved a dispute of the amount of damages claimed

    2. Any allegations to which no answer is required (or allowed) shall be taken as denied.

### (e) Consistency of Pleadings - Concise and Direct

    (1) Each allegation shall be Direct and Concise (no technical forms of pleadings/motions required).

    (2) A Pleader may state as many separate claims as it wants in the pleadings:

        a. Claims may be in one count or defense, or as separate ones

        b. A relationship between the claims is not necessary

        c. If one statement is improper, it does not negate the entire pleading (i.e. only the improper allegation will be negated).

### (f) Construction of Pleadings: Pleadings shall be construed so as to promote *"Substantial Justice"*

# RULE 9:  Pleading Special Matters

## (a) Capacity
1. There is no need to show capacity or authority to sue (under Rule 17(b)), unless there is a need to show Jurisdictional capacity.
2. If a party wants to raise a capacity issue, it must do so in a *specific negative* allegation (which must be stated with <u>particularity</u>, (i.e. with a specific factual foundation)).

## (b) Fraud, Mistake, Condition of Mind –
1. <u>Accusations of Fraud, Mistake</u> - must be stated with *particularity* (i.e. with a Specific factual foundation).
2. <u>Accusations of Malice, Intent, Knowledge, and Conditions of Mind</u> - may be alleged *generally*.

## (c) Conditions Precedent:
1. A Denial that a Condition Precedent has not been fulfilled must be stated with *particularity*.
2. An allegation that a Condition Precedent was performed may be alleged *generally*.

## (d) Official Document or Act - It is sufficient to simply say that it was done in compliance with the law.

## (e) Judgment - Domestic or foreign court judgments are sufficient to aver a judgment or decision. There is no need to describe the jurisdiction of the court.

## (f) Time and Place - To test sufficiency of pleadings averments of time and place are material, and should be treated like other averments of material matter.

## (g) Special Damages - must be *specifically* stated.

## (h) Admiralty and Maritime Claims - A case that includes an admiralty or maritime claim within this subdivision is an admiralty case within 28 U.S.C. §1292(a)(3).

# RULE 10: Form Of Pleadings

### (a) Captions; Names of Parties
    i. Every pleading requires a caption with:
        1. Name Of Court
        2. Title of Action
        3. File number (docket number)
        4. Type of pleading (see 7(a); ex: answer, complaint)
        5. Name of first party on each side
    ii. If the pleading is a **complaint** it must *also* include the names of <u>all</u> parties.

### (b) Separate Statements
    1. All allegations (claims/defenses) shall be made in NUMBERED paragraphs.
    2. Each paragraph shall be limited to a single set of circumstances (or whenever needed for clarity).
    3. In later paragraphs or pleadings, paragraphs may be referred to by paragraph number.

### (c) Adoption by Reference:
    1. Statements in a pleading may be adopted by reference in:
        a. Other parts of the pleadings
    or b. In different pleadings
    or c. In motions
    2. An exhibit is a part of a pleading for all purposes

# RULE 11:  Signing Pleadings

## (a) Signature

1. Signature must be made <u>by the lawyer</u>; if there is no lawyer, the pleader must sign.
2. The signer must include his address and telephone number.
3. There is no need to accompany pleadings with an affidavit (unless specifically provided for by another rule or statute)
4. If the signature is missing, the court may *strike* the pleadings, unless it is signed promptly after such omission is brought to the pleader's attention.

## (b) Representations to Court

A <u>signature</u> implies that, to best of the signer's knowledge, with *reasonable inquiry*, the pleading is:

> (1) Made with a <u>Proper Purpose</u> - not to harass or cause unnecessary cost or delay

> and (2) <u>Warranted by *Existing Law*</u> (or a <u>non-frivolous</u> argument to change existing law)

> and (3) <u>Well grounded in fact</u> - likely to be reasonably supported by facts

> and (4) <u>Based on Evidence</u> - Denials of factual contentions are based on evidence or reasonably based on lack of belief/information.

## (c) Sanctions - If Rule 11(b) is violated, the court may impose sanctions to lawyers/signers:

> (1) <u>How Sanctions are Initiated:</u>

>> (A) **By Motion**:

>>> 1. Motion for Sanctions must be made separately from other motions.
>>> 2. The motion must state violation of Rule 11(b).
>>> 3. The motion may only be filed if the pleading is not corrected within <u>21 Days</u> of service.
>>> 4. The court may award the winner reasonable expenses and fees incurred in making or opposing the motion.
>>> 5. Law firms will be held jointly liable  - *absent exceptional circumstances*.

(B) **On Court's Initiative**: If the court initiates the sanctions (by Order to Show Cause), the burden of proof will fall on the pleader to show that it is not in violation.

(2) <u>Limitation of Sanctions</u>: Sanctions shall be limited to what is *"sufficient to deter repetition"* of the conduct. This may include:

    i. Non-monetary damages (ex: Equitable damages)

    ii. Penalties paid to the court

    iii. Payment of another party's expenses/lawyer's fees

    iv. <u>Money damages shall not be awarded for:</u>

        (A) Violations of 11(b)(2) (pleading not warranted by law) against represented party

        (B) When initiated by Court (Rule 11(c)(1)(B)), unless the Court issues an Order to Show Cause *before* either:

            1. A Voluntary Dismissal (made by or against a party (or attorney) to be sanctioned)

           or 2. A Settlement of Claims (made by or against a party (or attorney) to be sanctioned)

(3) <u>Order:</u> Court shall prescribe conduct and basis for sanction.

**(d) Inapplicability to Discovery** - Rule 11 does not apply to:

    1. Disclosures

    2. Discovery requests

    3. Responses

    4. Objections

    5. Motions subject to provisions in Rules 26 – 37

# RULE 12:   Objections and Defenses

## (a) Time Frame for Parties to Respond

    (1) <u>Answer and Complaint</u>: Unless a U.S. statute supersedes, the *Answer* must be served:

        (A) *If Summons Served:* the answer must be served within <u>20 days</u> after service (extended if out-of-state).

        (B) *If Service Waived:* the answer must be served within <u>60 days</u> after request for waiver is *sent* (90 if outside of the U.S.).

    (2) <u>Cross-claims/Counterclaims</u>:

        a. <u>Answer to a Cross-claim</u>: If the Answer is in response to a Cross-Claim, $\pi$ has <u>20 days</u> from the date the cross-claim was served.

        b. <u>Response to a Counterclaim</u>: The $\pi$ shall reply to a Counterclaim:

            1. Within <u>20 Days</u> after service of Defendant's answer

            2. Within <u>20 Days</u> after service of a court order, if $\pi$'s reply is ordered by the court (unless the order directs otherwise)

    (3) <u>Extension for U.S.</u>: If the U.S. is a party, it shall have <u>60 days</u> to answer.

    (4) <u>Exceptions to Time Limit</u>: The time limitations above will not apply in the following cases:

        (A) *If a Court denies the motion or postpones disposition -* then the Answer is due within <u>10 days</u> after Court notifies of decision to proceed

      or (B) *If a Court grants motion for a more definite statement -* then within <u>10 days</u> after receipt of $\pi$'s revised pleadings

**(b) How Presented:**
    i. All Defenses must be made in answer, *except for*:
        (1) Motion for lack of <u>Subject Matter Jurisdiction</u>
        (2) Motion for lack of <u>Personal Jurisdiction</u>
        (3) Motion for <u>improper venue</u>
        (4) Motion for <u>insufficiency of process</u>
        (5) Motion for <u>insufficiency of service</u> of process
        (6) Motion for <u>failure to state a valid claim</u> upon which relief
            can be granted
        (7) Motion for <u>failure to join a party</u> under Rule 19
        8. Other defenses to claims not requiring an answer
    ii. The above defenses are made in a pre-answer motion.
    iii. <u>Implied Motion for Summary Judgment:</u>
        1. A 12(b)(6) motion shall be treated as a motion for Summary
            Judgment (as per Rule 56) if:
            a. The 12(b)(6) motion is made (failure to state a claim).
        and b. Matters outside the pleading are presented to the
            court (which are not excluded by the court).
        2. In such a case, all parties shall be given a reasonable
            opportunity to present all material pertinent to such a
            motion (as per Rule 56).
    iv. <u>Consolidated Defense:</u> All 12(b) motions must be made **before**
        **pleadings** if a *"consolidated defense"* is used (as per Rule 12(g),
        below).
    v. Where no response to a Pleading is requires, the above defenses
        may be made at trial.

**(c) Motion for Judgment on the Pleadings**
    1. This motion may be made after the pleadings if it does not delay
        the trial.
    2. If matters outside pleadings are presented and accepted by court,
        this becomes a Rule 56 motion for summary judgment (and all
        parties shall be given a reasonable opportunity to present all material pertinent
        to such a motion (as per Rule 56)).

**(d) Preliminary Hearings** on any motions (under 12(b)(1)-(7)) shall be
    granted upon the request of any party, unless the judge decides to
    defer the hearing until trial.

**(e) Motion for More Definite Statement:**

1. This motion may be made if π's pleadings are too vague/ambiguous so that Defendant cannot reasonably frame a response.
2. The motion must point out the defects in π's pleadings.
3. If granted, the π must re-plead within <u>10 days</u> of the notice of motion (otherwise the court may strike pleadings or make any other order).

**(f) Motion to Strike** - the court may order to Strike something from the pleadings if it contains:
   1. Insufficient defenses
   2. Redundancies
   3. Immaterialities
   4. Scandalous matter

**(g) Consolidating Defense** –
   (1) A party can make a Consolidated Defense in order to join motions under this rule with any other motions available to the Defendant.
   (2) If this motion is made, any available Rule 12(b) defenses that are omitted will be deemed to be <u>waived</u> (unless allowed by 12(h)).

**(h) Waiver or Preservation of Defenses** –
   (1) Objection to
        a. Lack of <u>Personal Jurisdiction</u> (Rule 12(b)(2))
        or b. Improper <u>Venue</u> (Rule 12(b)(3))
        or c. Insufficiency of <u>Process</u> (Rule 12(b)(4))
        or d. Insufficiency of <u>Service</u> (Rule 12(b)(5)) <u>will be **waived if:**</u>
             (A) Omitted from Consolidated of motions (12(g)) (i.e. if you make one, you must make all)
             or (B) Not in Responsive Pleadings, in a motion (as per 12(b)), or in an amendment (under 15(a))
   (2) <u>Motions which may be made at trial or in pleadings:</u>
        a. Failure to sate a valid Claim (Rule 12(b)(6))
        b. Failure to Join a third party under Rule 19 (Rule 12(b)(7))
   (3) Motion for <u>Lack of Subject Matter Jurisdiction</u> (Rule 12(b)(1)) may be made AT ANY TIME (even after judgment).

# RULE 13: Counterclaims / Cross-claims

**(a) Compulsory Counterclaims**
  i. A *"Compulsory Counterclaim"* is any RELATED claim -
      "arising out of" the initial action *(i.e. they must arise out of the "same transaction or occurrence").*
  ii. Compulsory Counterclaims <u>MUST</u> be joined.
  iii. Any third parties involved must have Personal Jurisdiction
  iv. The Counterclaim must be stated in the pleading *unless:*
      (1) The claim is already subject to another pending action
      (2) The Defendant brings the suit by attachment or process
          without the Court's jurisdiction.

**(b) Permissive Counterclaims**
  1. A *"Permissive Counterclaim"* is <u>any</u> claim <u>*against*</u> an <u>*opposing party*</u> (not a new party) which is not related to action.
  2. Permissive Counterclaims MUST BE STATED IN PLEADINGS

**(c) Counterclaims exceeding Opposing Claims** – Counterclaims may
    seek more relief or different relief than the original claims that the
    opposing party had sought.

**(d) Counterclaims against the U.S.** - These rules shall not enlarge the
    present limits, (fixed by statute) of asserting Counterclaims against the
    U.S. government.

**(e) Post-Pleading Counterclaims** - may be presented as a *Counterclaim*
    in a *Supplemental Pleading*, if the Court allows.

**(f) Omitted Counterclaim** - a pleader may obtain leave of court, to
    Counterclaim by amending the pleading, only if it is omitted by
      1. Oversight
    or 2. Inadvertence
    or 3. Excusable neglect
    or 4. *When justice so requires.*

**(g) Cross-claims against a Co-Party** - are usually considered permissive.
  1. Guarantors <u>Same Transaction</u>:  May allow Cross-claim against a co-party for a claim either:
      a. *Arising out of the same transaction or occurrence* of *either*:
          1. The original action
          or 2. A Counterclaim
      or b. Relating to any property subject to the original action
  2. <u>Indemnity</u>: Cross-claims may include a claim to a co-party to indemnify the claimant for all or part of the liability arising out of the action.

**(h) Joinder of Additional Parties** - parties may be joined in Counterclaims and Cross-claims (pursuant to Rules 19 and 20).

**(i) Separate Trials; Separate Judgments** - Judgment on a Cross-Claim or Counterclaim may be made in accordance with Rule 54(b) (even if the claims of the opposing party have been dismissed or otherwise disposed of) if:
  1. A Court orders separate trials pursuant to Rule 42(b)
  and 2. The Court has jurisdiction to do so.

# RULE 14: Third Party Practice

### (a) When Defendant May Bring a Third Party

1. At any time <u>after</u> the commencement of an action, the Defendant may become a "third party π" by serving a Complaint on a third party (who is not in the original action). This happens when the Defendant feels that the third party is liable to *indemnify* the Defendant for any judgment (ex: insurance company or surety).

2. If the Defendant serves the third party no later than <u>10 days</u> after serving its original Answer. No "leave of court" is needed to serve the third party. After 10 days, the Defendant must get "leave of court" by filing a motion with notice to all parties.

3. The third party is then known as a "Third Party Defendant" and the Defendant is known as a "Third Party Plaintiff."

4. Third Party Defendant's options in response to Defendant's pleadings:

    a. <u>Answer</u> - third may assert any defenses which the Defendant may have to π's claim.

    b. <u>Counterclaim against π</u> - *arising out of the same transaction or occurrence* of π's claim against Defendant.

    c. <u>Cross-claims against Defendant</u>

5. π may Counterclaim against third

6. Any party may move to:

    a. Strike third party claim

    or b. Sever the claim

    or c. Separate trial

7. A third party may bring in a 4th party who may also be liable to the Defendant or the third party (Note: Complete diversity is not needed for third party.)

8. Admiralty and Maritime Claims   \*\*\*

### (b) When π may bring a third party: When a Counterclaim is made against the π, the π may bring in a third party just as the Defendant (under Rule 14(a)).

### (c) Admiralty and Maritime Claims

\*\*\*

# RULE 15: Amending Pleadings

**(a) Amendments:**
    1. Parties have a *right* to 1 amendment:
        a. Before the answer or responding pleading is served.
        b. In a non-responsive pleading, <u>20 days</u> after the pleading is
           served.
    2. Otherwise, amending party must:
        a. Request a *"leave of court"* to amend the pleading (Court must
           consent when "*justice so requires*")
    or b. Obtain <u>written consent</u> from the adverse parties
    3. <u>Answering Amendments</u> - must be done within the *longer of:*
        a. <u>10 days</u> after service of the amendment
    or b. The time remaining within the original 20 day response
           period (from the initial pleading)

**(b) Amendments to Conform to the Evidence**
    1. Issues *expressly* or *impliedly* consented to by parties are
       considered to have been raised in pleadings (although they never
       were).
    2. Parties may raise a *Motion to Amend* the Pleadings (to conform to
       the evidence) at any time, <u>even after judgment</u>.
    3. If a party objects to <u>amendments, new evidence,</u> or <u>issues not</u>
       <u>explicitly included in pleadings</u>, the court may still grant/allow
       if it will *promote justice* (and the other party cannot show prejudice).
    4. The court may grant a continuance to allow the objecting party to
       meet the evidence.

**(c) Relation Back of Amendments:** Amendments will be considered to
    relate back to date of the original pleading if:
        (1) <u>Permitted by the law</u> providing for the Statute of
           Limitations in the case.
    or (2) They are <u>related to the original claims</u> (i.e. arising out of the
           same conduct, transaction, or occurrence)

or (3) There were <u>misidentified parties</u> in original claim. Such amendments will relate back to date of pleading only upon reasonable notice if:

> (A) A Party has received notice of the action and will not be prejudiced in maintaining a defense on the merits.

> and (B) The Party knew or should have known that the action would have been taken against her, *but for* the fact that there was a mistake as to her actual identity.

## (d) Supplemental Pleadings:

1. Upon Motion, Pleadings may be <u>amended for events</u> occurring *after* service of the original pleadings if:

   a. Reasonable notice is given

   and b. The terms are just

2. Supplemental Pleadings must set forth the transactions or events that have happened since the date of the original pleading was drafted.

3. Permission to supplement a pleading may be granted, even though the original pleading has a defective statement claiming relief or defense.

4. If the court deems it advisable, it may order the opposing party to respond within a specified time.

# RULE 16: Pretrial Conference

## (a) Objectives:  A Court may order (at its discretion) that parties appear for a conference to:

(1) Expedite disposition of an action

or (2) Establish early controls, so that the case is not "protracted" from lack of management

or (3) Discourage wasteful pre-trial activities

or (4) Improve the quality of trial with more thorough preparation

or (5) Facilitate Settlement of the case

**(b) Scheduling and Planning**
1. If the court requires, the Judge shall enter a <u>Scheduling Order</u> (upon consultation w the parties), limiting the time to:
   (1) Join other parties and Amend pleadings
   (2) File Motions
   (3) Complete discovery
   (4) Modify:
      a. Disclosure times created in 26(f) Conference
      b. The extent of discovery permitted
   (5) Include dates for pre-trial conferences and trial dates (Optional)
   (6) Include any other appropriate matters under the circumstances
2. The Order shall be made ASAP, AFTER the Rule 26(f) ~~Conf~~ Conference, yet no more than:
   a. <u>120 days</u> after the complaint has been served
and b. <u>90 days</u> after Defendant has made an appearance
3. The Schedule may only be modified by *either* a:
   a. Leave of court
and b. Showing of good cause
and c. Authorization by local rule

**(c) Subjects to be Discussed at Conference** - Participants may consider and take action regarding:
   (1) Formulation/Simplification of Issues to eliminate frivolous claims
   (2) Necessity/Desirability of amending pleadings
   (3) Possibility of obtaining Disclosure/Admissions to reduce factual disputes
   (4) Avoidance of unnecessary proof of evidence and limitations of evidence (pursuant to Federal Rules of Evidence)
   (5) Appropriateness/Timing of a Rule 56 Summary Judgment Motion.
   (6) Control/Scheduling of discovery
   (7) Identification of Witnesses/Documents
   (8) Advisability of referring matters to a Magistrate
   (9) Settlement and use of ADR (Alternate Dispute Resolution)
   (10) Form or Substance of the pre-trial order
   (11) Disposition of pending motions
   (12) Need for adopting special procedures for specific complex issues (or unusual proof problems)
   (13) Orders for separate trials (as per Rule 42(b))

(14) Orders to present certain evidence early (to facilitate early judgments (pursuant to Rule 50(a) and 52(c))

(15) Orders establishing a reasonable time limit for presenting evidence

(16) Other matters to facilitate a just, speedy, inexpensive disposition of the action

17) Prepare a schedule for
    a. Exchanging briefs
    b. Further conferences
    c. Trial

18. Attempt to settle the case:
    a. The Court may require that a party or representative be present or *reasonably available* by phone (to consider settling the dispute).
    b. At least one of each party's attorney must be present at any pre-trial conference, and must have the authority to:
        1. Enter into stipulations
        2. Make admissions (regarding matter anticipated to be discussed)

### (d) Final Pretrial Conference

1. Shall be held as close to the trial date as reasonably possible.
2. Shall discuss trial plans, including admission of evidence.
3. At least one attorney per party who will be at the trial must appear.

### (e) Pretrial Orders

1. After each conference, an order shall be filed, reciting the action taken at the conference.
2. Orders may only be modified by a subsequent order.
3. Orders after a Final Pre-Trial Conference may only be modified to prevent a *manifest injustice*.

### (f) Sanctions:  Rule 37 sanctions will be invoked if:

1. A Party or its attorney fails to obey a scheduling order
2. A Party or its attorney comes unprepared to participate in the conference.
3. There is no good faith effort of participation by a party.

# *IV. Parties*

## RULE 17: Parties

**(a) Real Party in Interest**

    1. Every action shall be prosecuted in the name of the real party in interest

        a. <u>A trustee or bailee</u> may sue on behalf of a beneficiary without joining the beneficiary.

        b. <u>The U.S.</u> may sue on behalf of a beneficiary if a statute so provides.

    2. An action cannot be dismissed because it was not originally brought in the name of the interested party.

        a. A Court may dismiss a case if it gave $\pi$ *reasonable time* for an interested party to *"ratify"* the action (bring it in its name).

        b. Once an interested party ratifies an action, the action will be considered to have been commenced at the time the original party brought the action.

**(b) Capacity to Sue or be Sued** - Capacity to sue shall be determined:

        a. <u>For an Individual</u>: by the law in the party's state of *<u>domicile</u>*

        b. <u>For a Corporation</u>: by the law in the state in which it was *<u>organized</u>*

        c. <u>For all other cases</u>: by the law in the state of the District Court (i.e. Forum State) *<u>unless</u>*:

            (1) For a <u>Partnership</u> or <u>Unincorporated Association</u>; it may sue in its common name for actions involving Federal rights (only if it has <u>no</u> capacity to sue under state law).

            (2) 28 USC §754 and §959(a) govern the capacity of a receiver appointed by the U.S..

**(c) Infants or Incompetent Persons**

    1. *<u>Those with Representatives</u>: Infants or Incompetents with general guardians, fiduciaries, or representatives*:  A representative may sue or be sued on behalf of the infant or incompetent person.

    2. *<u>Those without Representatives</u>: Infants/Incompetents without general guardians, etc.:* The court shall appoint a representative or *"guardian ad litem"* to represent the infant or incompetent in court.

# RULE 18: Joinder of Claims & Remedies

**(a) Joinder of Claims** - A party may join *as many* independent or alternate claims as it has against an **opposing** parties. These include:

> 1. Original claims
> 2. Counterclaims
> 3. Cross-claims
> 4. third party claims

**(b) Joinder of Remedies** -  Whenever a claim is dependent on the outcome of a claim in another action, the two actions may be joined into a single action.

# RULE 19: Compulsory Joinder

**(a) Persons To Be Joined** (if feasible)
> 1. <u>Requirements</u>:
>> a. Joined parties must be subject to <u>Personal Jurisdiction</u>
>> and b. Joinder cannot destroy SMJ (diversity)
> 2. <u>A Third Party MUST be joined if</u>:
>> (1) *Complete relief* cannot be accorded among the present parties without joining the third party.
>> or (2) The third party claims a *related interest* in the action, and its absence from the suit may:
>>> (i)  Impair or Impede its ability to protect that interest.
>>> or (ii) Leave any of the present parties subject to <u>double liability</u> or <u>inconsistent verdicts</u>.
> 3. If a third party refuses to be a $\pi$, he may, upon the Court's discretion, be made:
>> a. A Defendant
>> or b. An *Involuntary* $\pi$

4. If a third party objects to venue, and his presence makes venue improper, the joinder will be dismissed (and the entire case itself will also be dismissed if third party is considered an "*indispensable party*").

## (b) Determination by Court Whenever Joinder is Not Feasible

1. The Court may determine that a third party is "*indispensable*," and dismiss the case if he cannot be joined.
2. An "Indispensable Party" is a party who in, "*in equity or in conscience*" the case should not proceed without.

3. FACTORS CONSIDERED (to determine if third party is "indispensable"):
   a. The Extent of prejudices to the present Party's that the third party's absence may bring
   b. The Extent that Prejudices may be avoided or reduced by other means
   c. The Adequacy of judgment without the third party
   d. Whether the $\pi$ will have an adequate remedy if the case were dismissed for non-joinder.

# RULE 20: Permissive Joinder of Parties

## (a) Permissive Joinder –

1. All persons may join as a $\pi$ or a Defendant, if they assert or are subject to any *right to relief* (ex: Indemnity) which *both*:
   a. Arises out of the same transaction or occurrence (or series of transactions or occurrences)
   and b. Has a question of law or fact common to all co-parties in the action (i.e. if you are guilty of negligence and you think a third party is contributorily negligent, you can join her).
2. There is no need for all $\pi$s or Ds to seek all claims of relief being claimed in the action; judgment will be accorded as per each party's respective rights or liabilities.

**(b) Separate Trials** -  The Court may order separate trials or make *other such orders* to prevent:

1. A party from being embarrassed

or 2. Delay

or 3. Prejudice

or 4. A party from incurring undue expense from the inclusion of a third party, if no claims exists between the parties.


# RULE 21: Misjoinder and Non-Joinder of Parties

1. Misjoinder is NOT a ground for dismissal of an action.
2. Parties may be dropped or added at any stage of the action by:
   a. Motion
   or b. Courts initiative
3. Any claim against a party may be severed and proceeded with separately (see Rule 42).


# RULE 22: Interpleader

("Rule Interpleader" - requires Complete Diversity)

(1) Interpleader is required if the $\pi$ might be exposed to double liability.
   a. Interpleader may take place, even though:
      1. There is no common origin of causes
      or 2. The actions are not identical - but are adverse & independent actions
   b. Defendant may also interplead if he might be held to double liability.
(2) This remedy does not supersede 28 USC §1335, §1397, or §2361.

# RULE 23: Class Actions

**(a) Prerequisites to a Class Action** - one or more members of a class may sue or be sued as representative parties IF:

    (1) "Numerosity": The class is so large that the joinder of all members is impracticable

and (2) "Commonality": There is a common question of law or fact involved

and (3) "Typicality": claims or defenses of the representative parties are typical of the rest of the class

and (4) "Adequacy": The Representative parties will adequately and fairly protect the class' interests

**(b) Class Actions Maintainable:**

i. A Class Action will be maintained if 23(a) is satisfied, AND, *either:*

    (1) Separate actions by individual members would create a risk of

        (A) *Inconsistent/Varying adjudications*, which would establish incompatible standards of conduct for the opposing party (mostly used in property actions, nuisance, or reward cases)

    or (B) Adjudication for an individual member which would *substantially* impair or impede other members from taking action or protecting themselves (mostly for declaratory judgments, injunctions)

    or (2) The opposing party has acted similarly adverse to the entire class

    or (3) The court finds that (mostly for damages)

        a. The facts common to class is *predominate over* the facts specific to each individual

     and b. A class action would be the best way for *fair and efficient* adjudication

ii. Pertinent consideration which court must weigh:

    (A) The *Interest of members* to individually control their own cases

    (B) The *Extent and nature of litigation* involved

    (C) The *Desirability of concentrating the litigation* in a particular forum

(D) The *Difficulties likely to be encountered* in managing the class action (ex: expenses)

**(c) Order determining whether Class Action shall be maintained:**
  (1) Certification
    a. Determination of allowing a class action shall be made *as soon as practicable*.
    b. An order may be *conditional*, and may be later *altered or amended* before a decision is made on the merits.
  (2) Notice Requirements for 23(b)(3) Actions:
    i. The Court shall determine the best method of notifying class members.
    ii. Notice must advise each member that:
        (A) The Court will exclude the member from the class upon a member's request (before the specified date)
      and (B) The judgment will include all members who do not request exclusion
      and (C) Any member who does not request exclusion *may* enter an appearance through counsel.
  (3) Judgment:
    a. *Judgments over Class Actions under (b)(1) and (b)(2)* - shall apply to all people that the court finds to be members of the class.
    b. *Judgments over Class Actions under (b)(3)* - shall apply to all people which the court finds to be members of the class if:
        1. The members received appropriate notice of the action
      and 2. The members did not request exclusion from the class
  (4) Partial Class Actions may be brought if:
    (A) The Class Action may be brought only with respect to particular issues of an action
    or (B) A class may be subdivided into subclasses (each subclass shall be treated as a separate class)

**(d) Orders in Conduct of Actions:**

    i. The court may make appropriate orders, in its discretion, to:
        (1) Prescribe measures to prevent due repetition or complication
        (2) Require specific methods of notice
        (3) Impose conditions on representative parties
        (4) Require that pleadings be amended to represent class
        (5) Determine the course of Proceedings and Procedural matters
    ii. <u>Rules:</u>
        a. Such orders may be combined with the Rule 16 provisions
        b. Such orders may be amended as court sees fit

**(e) Dismissal or Compromise** (settlement) - To dismiss or settle a class action suit, the parties must:
    1. Obtain court's approval
and 2. Give notice to all class members (as court directs)

**(f) Appeals:**
    1. A court of appeals may permit an appeal from a district court order that grants or denies class action certification.
    2. <u>Time:</u>  Application for an appeal must be made within 10 days after entry of the order denying or granting the certification.
    3. <u>Stay of Proceedings:</u>  An appeal <u>does not</u> stay the District Court proceedings unless ordered by either:
        a.  The district court judge
        b.  The court of appeals

# RULE 23.1: Derivative Actions by Shareholders

a. In a derivative action brought by one or more shareholders to enforce a right of a corporation, shareholders must prepare a complaint, alleging that:

    (1) The $\pi$ was a shareholder

        a. At the time of the transaction $\pi$ is complaining about

      or b. After the transaction, and $\pi$'s shares devolved on the $\pi$ by operation of law

  and (2) The action is not a collusive one to confer jurisdiction in a Federal Court, in which it otherwise may NOT have such jurisdiction

    3. The efforts (if any) made by $\pi$ to obtain a remedy directly with the Corp. directors/officers/shareholders *(must be stated with particularity)*.

    4. The reasons why $\pi$'s efforts to remedy the situation failed

b. Derivative action may not be maintained if it appears that $\pi$ does not adequately represent the interests of class (shareholders, members, and other similarly situated members).

c. <u>Settlements and compromises</u>

    1. The court must approve proposed settlements

    2. Class representatives must notify the class of any settlement (notification to be given in a manner proposed by court)

# RULE 23.2: Actions Relating to Unincorporated Associations

Actions brought by or against an unincorporated associations may only be maintained if it appears that the representatives will fairly and adequately represent the entire class.

# RULE 24: Intervention

### (a) Intervention of Right
    i. Anyone may intervene (upon <u>timely</u> application) in an action when:
        (1) A U.S. Statute allows
      or (2) The Applicant claims a *direct* interest in a <u>*related*</u>
           <u>*property/transaction*</u> subject to adjudication, <u>but only if:</u>
           a. The Applicant's interest isn't already properly
              represented in the case.
         or b. The Applicant has a direct "<u>*significantly*</u>
             <u>*protectable*</u>" interest at stake
        and c. Non-intervention will impair/impede the applicant's
            ability to protect that interest
    ii. A party may not intervene if <u>Complete Diversity</u> will not be
       maintained.

### (b) Permissive Intervention
    i. Intervention will be permitted if:
        (1) A U.S. Statute allows
      or (2) The Applicant's claim is related to the <u>main action</u> by
           question of law or fact.
    ii. The court has discretion, and should weigh any <u>delays &</u>
       <u>prejudices</u> to the original parties (resulting from the intervention).

### (c) Procedure - *Motion to Intervene:*
    1. The Intervening party shall serve a *Motion to Intervene* (as per Rule
       5).
    2. <u>Requirements of Motion to Intervene</u> - the motion must:
       a. State the grounds for intervention
     and b. Be accompanied by a pleading describing the claim or
         defense for which intervention is sought.
    3. The same procedure shall be followed when a U.S. statute
       provides for a right to intervene.
    4. If an action involves the constitutionality of an act of Congress,
       the Court shall notify the U.S. Attorney General (if a U.S.
       officer/agent is not already a party).
    5. If an action involves the constitutionality of a State law, the
       Court shall notify the State Attorney General (if a state
       officer/agent is not already a party).

# RULE 25: Substitution of Parties

**(a) Death:**
>    (1) <u>Death of a Party</u>
>> a. If a party dies, and his claim is not extinguished, a *Motion for Substitution* may be made by:
>>> 1. Any other party of the suit
>>> or 2. The successors or representatives of the deceased.
>> b. A Motion for Substitution must be made within <u>90 days</u> of record of the party's death.
>> c. Notice of hearing and motion shall be served on all parties and involved non-parties (pursuant to Rule 4 and 5).
>    (2) <u>Death with Multiple Parties</u> - If there are multiple parties on either side and one party dies, the suit will not be dismissed, and any liability of the claim will remain with the survivors.

**(b) Incompetency**
>    1. If a party becomes incompetent, the court may allow the suit to continue in the name of a representative of the incompetent person.
>    2. A Motion for Substitution must be made within <u>90 days</u> of record of party's Incompetency.
>    3. The motion and notice of hearing shall be served on all parties and involved non-parties (pursuant to Rule 4 and 5).

**(c) Transfer of Interest**
>    1. If there is a transfer of interest:
>> a. The original party may continue in the action.
>> or b. The transferee may substitute the original party.
>> or c. The transferee may be joined with the original party.
>> or d. The court may direct that the transferee substitute the original party.
>    2. Motion for Substitution must be made within <u>90 days</u> of record of party's transfer.
>    3. Notice of hearing and motion shall be served on all parties and involved non-parties (pursuant to Rule 4 and 5).

**(d) Public Officers**

   (1) <u>Death of Public Officer - *Automatic Substitution*</u>:
       a. If a Public Officer acting in a suit in an official capacity dies or leaves office, the officer's successor shall automatically be substituted.
       b. Further proceedings in the action shall be made in the name of the substituted party.
       c. An order of substitution may be entered at any time.
       d. Failure to make an order of substitution will <u>*not*</u> affect the substitution.

   (2) <u>Title</u>:  An officer suing or being sued in an official capacity may be described by his official title rather than his name, unless a court requires that the officer's name be added to the suit.

# *V. DISCOVERY AND DEPOSITIONS*

## RULE 26: General Provisions Governing Discovery

**(a) Required Disclosures** - Methods to discover:

(1) Initial Disclosure
    i. A must provide (without waiting for a discovery request):
        (A) **People** (name, address, phone (if available), and subject matter of the information) likely to have discoverable information (relevant to disputed facts alleged with particularity in the pleadings)
        (B) Relevant **Documents**, data, and *"tangible things"* that are in the <u>possession</u>, <u>custody</u>, or <u>control</u> of the party (relevant to disputed facts alleged with particularity in the pleadings)
        (C) **Materials** from which computation of damages arose, *unless* <u>privileged</u> or <u>protected</u>
        (D) **Insurance Agreements** which may indemnify or pay part of judgment
    ii. <u>Exceptions</u>: The Initial Disclosure rules *do not apply*:
        1. If the parties stipulate otherwise
        2. If the court orders otherwise
    iii. Disclosures shall be made within <u>10 days</u> after the meeting of the parties (pursuant to Rule 26(f)).
    iv. All *"reasonably available"* information must be submitted. It is <u>not</u> a valid excuse that:
        1. Investigations are not fully complete
      or 2. Opponents' discovery is insufficient
      or 3. Opponents failed to submit discovery

(2) Disclosure of Expert Testimony:
        (A) A party must disclose the identity of all expert witnesses who may be used at trial (to present evidence under rules 702, 703, and 705 of the Federal Rules of Evidence)
        (B) Experts must submit and sign a <u>written report</u> containing:
            1. A complete statement of *all* opinions which may be expressed at trial

and 2. The basis and reasons for the expert's opinion

and 3. Data and information on which the opinion is based

and 4. Exhibits to be used to support the opinion

and 5. Qualifications of the expert (including all publications within the past 10 years)

and 6. Compensation to be paid for the study or testifying

and 7. A listing of all previous cases in which the expert had testified (*either* at trial <u>or</u> deposition)

(C) The **due date** of expert disclosures is (unless the court changes):

    1. <u>Initial Expert Testimony:</u> At least <u>90 days</u> before trial

    2. <u>Rebutting Expert Testimony</u> (responding to initial testimony): Within <u>30 Days</u> of the initial expert disclosure

(3) <u>Pretrial Disclosure</u> - for any evidence to be used at trial, a party shall disclose:

(A) The **name, address, phone** of each witness and the subject matter of their testimony (if not already provided), separately indicating which witnesses may appear trial and which may not.

(B) **Designation** of witnesses whose testimony is expected to be by deposition.

*exhibit list* (C) Appropriate **identification** of each document and exhibit, and summaries of evidence

D. <u>Other Disclosure Rules:</u>

    1. Pretrial disclosure must be submitted at least <u>30 days</u> before trial.

    2. Within <u>14 days</u> after pretrial disclosure, a party may file a list disclosing:

        (i) Any objections to the use of depositions

        (ii) Any objections to the admissibility of materials (with a reason for the objection)

    3. If objections are not made before <u>14 days</u>, they are deemed to be waived, unless excused for *good cause.*

(4) <u>Form of Disclosure; Filing</u> - All disclosures shall be:

    a. In writing

and b. Signed

and c. Served

and d. Promptly filed in court

(5) <u>Methods to Discover Additional Matter</u> – Discovery may be
obtained in *one or more* of the following ways:
   a. <u>Depositions</u> - oral or written  (Rules 27,28,30,31,32)
   b. <u>Interrogatories</u> - written  (Rule 33)
   c. <u>Production of Documents or Things</u>  (Rule 34)
   d. <u>Permission to Enter</u> - upon land or other property for
      inspection or other purposes
   e. <u>Examinations</u> - Physical and mental  (Rule 35)
   f. <u>Requests for Admissions</u>  (Rule 36)

## (b) Discovery Scope and Limits
### (1) In General
   a. A party may obtain discovery regarding any matter that is:
      1. Not privileged
   and 2. Relevant to the subject of the action or any party in the
      action
   b. If the information sought appears *reasonably calculated* to
      lead to the discovery of admissible evidence, there can
      be no grounds for objection to obtaining them.
### (2) Limitations
   a. Local Rules or Courts (by court order) may alter these rules
      by setting limits on the <u>length</u> and <u>number</u> of depositions
      and interrogatories, and the number of Rule 36 Requests
      for Admissions.
   b. Discovery shall be limited if the court determines that:
      (i) The discovery sought is:
         a. unreasonably cumulative or duplicative
      or b. obtainable from a more convenient or less
         expensive source
      or (ii) The party seeking discovery has an ample
         opportunity to obtain the information sought.
      or (iii) Such discovery would be unduly burdensome or
         expensive in comparison to:
         a. The needs of the case
         or b. The amount in controversy
         or c. The limitations on the parties' resources
         or d. The importance of the issues at stake in the
            litigation
         or e. The likely benefit of discovery

c. The court may act on its own initiative <u>or</u> pursuant to a motion to limit discovery.

**(3) Trial Preparation: Materials (work-product)**

    a. <u>Disclosure:</u> A party may obtain discovery gathered *by another party* only upon a showing that he:

        1. Has a *"substantial need"* for the materials to prepare his case

        and 2. Cannot obtain the *"substantial equivalent"* of the materials without *"undue hardship"*

    b. Disclosure is limited to materials themselves. Courts will protect another party's work-product (ex: conclusions, theories of recovery, strategies, etc.).

    c. If a party "previously made a statement" concerning the action or subject matter, he does not have to present a new one when obtaining another party's materials.

        1. <u>If the other party denies materials</u> - The party seeking discovery may:

            a. Move for a court order to obtain the other party's materials.

            and b. Apply for expenses incurred in relation to the motion (under Rule 37(a)(4)).

        2. A **"previously made statement"** <u>is</u>:

            (A) A written statement signed or adopted by the person making it

            (B) A recorded transcript or recording of an oral statement by the person making the "showing"

    d. In order to claim materials as "privileged" or to classify them as "trial-preparation material," a party must:

        i. Expressly claim the reason for protection

        and ii. Describe the nature of the documents and communications specifically enough to allow court to assess the applicability of the privilege or protection

**(4) Trial Preparation; Obtaining Expert Opinions:**

    (A) **Depositions:**

        1. Depositions of any person identified as an expert may be taken and may be used at trial.

        2. If an Expert Disclosure Report is required (by local rules), the deposition shall be conducted *after* the report is received.

    (B) **Other Party's Experts:**

A party may discover known facts, or opinions of
another party's experts (via deposition or interrogatory)
who are <u>not</u> expected to be used at trial, but only if
the party shows *exceptional circumstances* that
make it impractical to obtain the expert information
himself (i.e. by hiring his own expert).

(C) <u>The court shall require the party requesting the
information to pay the following</u> (unless manifest injustice will
result):

(i) A reasonable fee to the expert for her time spent in
responding to its discovery requests.

and (ii) A reasonable portion of the expert's fee to the
other party for the expert opinions obtained by him.

**(c) Protective Orders:**

i. Requirements for requesting a Protective Order:

a. <u>Motion</u> for protection must be made

b. Showing of <u>Good Cause</u>

c. Certification of <u>Good-Faith Effort</u> or attempt to settle the
matter without the court

ii. A court may make any order *which justice requires* to protect any
party from:

a. Annoyance

or b. Embarrassment

or c. Oppression

or d. Undue burden or expense

iii. Controls which courts may use to protect parties include *one or
more of the following*:

(1) That disclosure or discovery is not to be had

(2) Disclosure or discovery may be had only on *specified
terms and conditions*

(3) Discovery be had by a *certain method*

(4) Discovery scope be limited to *certain matters*,
prohibiting inquiry into other matters

(5) Discovery be conducted in the privacy of a court
designee

(6) Sealed depositions only to be opened by court order

(7) Trade secrets or confidentiality not to be revealed, or to
be revealed in a specified manner

(8) Parties file simultaneous specified documents and
information in sealed envelopes to be opened with a
court order

## (d) Sequence and Timing of Discovery

1. Unless the court or a local rule allows, or the parties agree, a party may not seek discovery from any source until after a meeting of the parties (pursuant to Rule 26(f))
2. The methods of discovery may be used in any order, unless the court grants a motion based on:
   - a. Injustice
   - or b. Inconvenience of parties or witnesses
   - or c. Delays to the other party's discovery

## (e) Supplementation of Disclosures and Responses

A party who responded to a discovery request is <u>required</u> to supplement it with new information if:

- (1) The party learns that the disclosed information/interrogatories are *incomplete* or *incorrect*, and new information has not been made known to other the other parties during discovery (or in subsequent writings)
- or (2) There were *incorrect* or *incomplete* depositions/interrogatories of an expert, for which reports are required (as per Rule 26(a))

## (f) Meeting of Parties:

i. <u>Rules:</u>
   - a. Parties shall meet at least <u>14 days</u> before scheduling a Rule 16(b) conference or order
   - b. <u>Parties shall discuss:</u>
      1. The nature and basis of claim
      2. Their defenses
      3. Possibilities for a prompt settlement
      4. Disclosure arrangements and the creation of a discovery plan
   - c. A court order or local rule may exempt the meeting

ii. <u>Discovery proposals shall include:</u>
   - (1) What changes should be made to rules
   - and (2) What subjects need discovery
   - and (3) Due dates and phases
   - and (4) Any protective orders needed

iii. All parties' attorneys are required to make a *good faith* effort in reaching an agreement.

iv. A discovery plan must be submitted within <u>10 days</u> after the meeting.

**(g) Signing of Disclosures, Discovery Requests, Responses, and Objections**

(1) <u>Certification of Disclosures:</u>

i. Every disclosure must be signed by at least one attorney (or the party if not represented) to be valid (recognized by the court).

ii. The signature is a certification that to the *best of his knowledge, information, and belief* (formed after reasonable inquiry), the disclosure is <u>complete and correct</u> (as of the time it was made).

(2) <u>Certification of Discovery Requests, Responses, or Objections:</u>

i. Every discovery request, response, or objection must be signed by at least one attorney (or the party if not represented) to be valid (recognized by the court).

ii. The signature is a certification that to the *best of his knowledge, information, and belief* (formed after reasonable inquiry), the request, response, or objection is:

(A) <u>Consistent with good faith and existing law</u> (including these rules) or a good faith argument to extend, modify, or reverse an existing law

(B) <u>Has a Proper Purpose</u> - it is not used for purposes such as harassment, delay, or to increase costs of litigation

(C) <u>Is not unreasonable or unduly burdensome or expensive</u> when considering:

1. The needs of the case

and 2. The discovery already obtained in the case

and 3. The amount in controversy

and 4. The importance of the issues at stake in the litigation

        iii. An unsigned request, response, or objection will be
             stricken (unless it is signed promptly after the omission is
             brought to the party's attention)

(3) <u>Sanctions:</u>
        i. If rules are violated, appropriate sanctions (such as in Rule
          11) will be imposed, either by:
            a. The court's own initiative
        or b. Motion by the opposing side
        ii. <u>Sanctions may include</u> an order to pay the amount of the
          reasonable expenses incurred because of the
          violation, including *reasonable attorney's fees.*

# RULE 27: Depositions Before Action Or Pending Appeal:

**(a) Before Action**

(1) *Petition* - A person desiring to obtain testimony of any matter
    before an action is filed may file a petition showing:
        a. That the petitioner expects to be a party to a valid cause
          of action, but is unable to bring it as of yet
        b. The subject matter of the expected action
        c. The petitioner's interest in the action
        d. The facts the petitioner hopes to establish with the
          proposed testimony
        e. The reasons for desiring to obtain testimony
        f. The names and descriptions of expected adverse parties
          (and their locations)
        g. The names of the people to be examined (to testify)
        h. The subject matter of the testimony expected to be
          elicited
        i. A request for an order authorizing the petitioner to take
          depositions as testimony

(2) *Notice and Service*
    a. After the petition filed, the petitioner shall serve a notice upon all named adverse parties, which includes:
        1. A copy of the petition
        2. A statement that the petitioner will apply to the court at the named place and time
    b. The notice must be served within <u>20 days</u> (pursuant to Rule 4(d)).
    c. If the notice cannot be served with *due diligence*, the court will:
        i. Order a specified method of publication or notice
        ii. Appoint a special attorney to represent the adverse parties if they do not have an attorney

(3) *Order and Examination* - If the court believes that delay of the testimony will cause an injustice, the court will:
    a. Make an order designating or describing people who may testify
    b. Specify the subject matter to be examined
    c. Specify method of testimony (Deposition or Interrogatories)

(4) *Use of Deposition* - A deposition may be used as testimony if:
    a. The action is related to the subject matter of the deposition
and b. It would be admissible evidence in the court of the state in which the deposition was taken.

## (b) Pending Appeal

1. If a case is pending appeal, but there is a chance it will return to the district court, a party may request "leave" to take depositions for use in the event of further proceedings in the district court.

2. A <u>motion for leave to take deposition</u> must be filed, including:
    (1) The names and addresses of people to be examined and the substance of testimony expected to be elicited
and (2) The reasons for requesting advance testimony

## (c) Perpetuation by Action - "This rule does not limit the power of a court to entertain an action to perpetuate testimony."

# RULE 28:  Persons Before Whom Depositions May Be Taken

**(a) Within the United States** - Depositions may be taken before *either:*
>     1. An officer "authorized to administer oaths by U.S. law"
> or 2. A person appointed by the court

**(b) In Foreign Countries** - Depositions may be taken *either:*
>     (1) Pursuant to any applicable treaty or convention
> or (2) Pursuant to a letter of request (no need to be "rogatory")
> or (3) On notice with an oath administrator authorized by U.S. law
>         or the foreign country's law
> or (4) With a person commissioned by the court

* * *

**(c) Disqualification for Interest** - A deposition may not be taken by any interested party, which includes
>     1. A fiduciary, attorney, employee, or relative of a party or the attorney
> or 2. Someone financially interested in the action

# RULE 29: Stipulations Regarding Discovery Procedure

Unless the court otherwise mandates, parties may agree *in writing* to:
>     (1) Provide for depositions, which may be taken before any person, at any time or any place.
> and (2) Modify procedures and limitations dictated by the Federal Rules (except extending time limits, which may only be extended by the court).

# <u>RULE 30</u>: Depositions Upon Oral Examination

**(a) When Leave Required for Depositions:**

    (1) A party may normally take depositions of anyone *without* leave of court.

    (2) <u>Leave of court is only required if</u>:

        (A) The Proposed deposition will result in more than <u>10</u> depositions (under Rule 30 or 31) by a party.

      or (B) The Person to be examined has already been deposed.

      or (C) A party requests to take a deposition before a Rule 26(f) discovery meeting, *unless a witness is leaving the country and will not be available later*

      or D. The person to be deposed is in prison

**(b) Notice of Examination**

    (1) <u>General Requirements</u>

        a. *Notice to Take Deposition:* The deposing party must give reasonable notice in writing to every other party in the action, stating:

            1. The **time and place** the deposition is to be held

            2. The **name and address** of each person to be examined (if known)

            3. If name not known, a **general description** sufficient to identify the person or a particular class the deponent belongs to (if the name and address are unknown)

        b. *Subpoena Duces Tecum:* If a subpoena duces tecum is to be served, notice must include the materials sought to be produced.

    (2) <u>Method of Recording</u>

        a. The notice shall state the method of deposition recording.

        b. Depositions may be recorded by sound, video, or stenograph.

        c. The party taking the deposition shall bear the cost of recording.

        d. Any party may request a transcript of a deposition.

(3) <u>Additional Recordings</u>
　　　　a. Any party may designate another type of recording (at their
　　　　　　 expense) *in addition to* regular recording.
　　　　b. Prior notice to the deponent and any other parties is
　　　　　　 required.
(4) <u>Deposition Requirements</u>
　　　　i. Depositions shall be conducted before a court-appointed
　　　　　　 officer (unless the parties agree otherwise)
　　　　ii. A deposition must begin with:
　　　　　　 (A) The officer's name and business address
　　　　 and (B) The date, time, and place of the deposition
　　　　 and (C) The name of the deponent
　　　　 and (D) The administration of deponent's oath
　　　　 and (E) An identification of all persons present
　　　　iii. If the deposition is not recorded stenographically, the
　　　　　　 officer shall repeat items (A), (B), and (C) at the
　　　　　　 beginning of each new tape.
　　　　iv. The appearance or demeanor of a deponent cannot be
　　　　　　 distorted via camera or recording techniques (ex:
　　　　　　 disguising voice).
　　　　v. At the end of the deposition, the officer shall:
　　　　　　 A. Say that the deposition is complete
　　　　 and B. Explain who will take custody of the record
　　　　 and C. Discuss any pertinent matters
(5) <u>Production of Documents</u>
　　　　Notice to a party deponent may be accompanied by a Rule
　　　　　　 34 request for documents and tangible things (which are
　　　　　　 to be brought to the deposition).
(6) <u>Depositions of Organizations</u>
　　　　a. A party may name a corporation or business as a deponent
　　　　　　 and reasonably describe the matters to be examined.
　　　　b. <u>The organization must</u>:
　　　　　　 1. Designate one or more officers, directors, or
　　　　　　　　 managers to testify on its behalf
　　　　　　 2. Describe what each deponent will testify about
　　　　c. A subpoena is used to notify a non-party organization
　　　　d. An organization's representative shall testify to "*all
　　　　　　 matters known or reasonably available to the
　　　　　　 organization.*"

(7) <u>Remote Depositions:</u>
>> a. Upon <u>written</u> agreement of the parties or court order, a party may use a telephone or other "remote electronic means" (ex: fax) to take a deposition.
>> b. Depositions will be considered to have been taken where the deponent is located.

## (c) Examination and Cross Examinations

> 1. The Examiner of a witness may proceed as provided for in the FRE Rules 103 and 615 for trial
> 2. The officer should put the witness under oath and record the testimony.
> 3. All objections regarding the following shall be noted on the record:
>> a. To the officer's qualifications
>> b. The manner of the recording
>> c. The evidence presented
>> d. Any other aspect of the examination proceeding
> 4. If written depositions are used, the answers shall be given to the officer (who then records them).

## (d) Schedule and Duration - Motion to Terminate or Limit Examination

> (1) <u>Objections:</u>
>> a. Objections during the deposition must be stated *concisely* and in a *non-argumentative* and *non-suggestive* manner.
>> b. A party may only instruct a deponent not to answer a question if it is necessary to:
>>> 1. Preserve a privilege
>>> or 2. Enforce a limitation
>>> or 3. Present a motion to terminate (as per Rule 30(d)(3))
> (2) <u>Time Limit</u>
>> a. The court (by local rule or by court order) may limit the time permitted to take a deposition, but it shall allow <u>extra time</u> if:
>>> 1. Extra time is needed for a *fair examination*
>>> or 2. The deponent (or another party) impedes or delays the examination
>> b. The court may impose sanctions on deponents that impede or needlessly delay a deposition.

(3) <u>Motion to Terminate Examination</u>
    a. At any time during a deposition, a party or deponent
        may move to terminate the examination or change its
        scope.
    b. <u>Grounds for motion</u>:
        1. Conducted in bad faith
        2. Unreasonably embarrassing, annoying, or
          oppressive
    c. The court (in the district in which the deposition is being
        held) can termination or limit the scope of a
        deposition.
    d. The deposition will be suspended until the court has
        time to review the motion.

**(e) Review by Witness** - If a party or deponent ask to *review* depositions
before their completion:
    1. The deponent will have <u>30 days</u> after receiving the transcript
        to make changes.
  and 2. The deponent must give reasons for changes.
  and 3. The deponent must sign.

**(f) Certification and Filing by Officer**
    (1) <u>The Certification Process</u>:
        a. The officer shall certify that the deposition was made under
          oath and was accurately transcribed
        b. The certification must be:
          1. <u>In writing</u>,
        and 2. <u>Sealed</u> in an envelope
        and 3. *Either:*
          a. <u>Filed</u> with the court
        or b. <u>Sent to an attorney</u> who shall protect it against
          loss, destruction, or tampering
        c. Any copies of produced information shall be annexed to the
          deposition.
        d. Copies of depositions shall be sent to any requesting parties
          upon "reasonable payment."
    (2) The officer shall retain stenographic notes or copies of the
        deposition recording.
    (3) The party taking the deposition shall give prompt notice of filing
        to all other parties.

**(g) Failure to Attend or Serve**
>  (1) If a <u>serving party</u> does not attend a deposition, she is responsible for reasonable fees and expenses of the other party and the deponent, *if a court so orders*.
>  (2) If a <u>witness</u> does not attend because the serving party fails to serve a subpoena, the serving party must pay reasonable expenses/fees for the other party's attorney showing up, *if a court so orders*.

# RULE 31: Depositions Upon Written Questions

**(a) Notice of Serving Questions**
>  (1) A party may normally use *written questions* for its deposition leave of court
>  (2) <u>Leave of court is only required if</u>:
>>  (A) The proposed deposition will result in more than <u>10</u> depositions (under Rules 30 and 31) by a party.
>>  or (B) The person to be examined has already been deposed.
>>  or (C) A party makes a request to take the deposition before the Rule 26(f) discovery meeting.
>>  or D. The person to be deposed is in prison.
>  (3) If a party wants to use *written questions* for its deposition, he must serve them to *every* party, stating:
>>  a. The name and address of person to answer them (if known)
>>  b. If the name is unknown, a description sufficient to describe the person or class he is a part of.
>>  c. The name and title of the officer taking the deposition.
>  4. Within <u>14 days</u> of service of questions, a party may serve **cross-questions** to all other parties.
>  5. Within <u>7 days</u> of being served cross-questions, a party may serve **redirect questions** to all other parties.
>  6. Within <u>7 days</u> of redirect-questions, a party may serve **recross-questions** upon all other parties.
>  7. Courts may change the above times for cause shown.

**(b) Officer to Prepare Record** - All questions and notices shall be copied and given to the recording officer.

**(c) Notice of Filing** - The party filing must promptly give notice of the filing to all other parties.

# RULE 32: Use of Depositions in Court

(a) **Use of Depositions** - Depositions (if admissible under the FRE) may be used in court for any of the following purposes:

> (1) To <u>contradict or impeach</u> the testimony of a deponent as a witness or other purposes allowed by the FRE.
>
> (2) As <u>testimony of an adverse party</u> or on behalf of an organization, *but only* to be used by an <u>*adverse*</u> party for any purpose.
>
> (3) As personal <u>testimony of a non-party</u> to be used by any party for any purpose, if the court finds that:
>> (A) The witness is dead
>>
>> or (B) The witness is too far (more than 100 miles from the place of trial, or outside of the U.S.), unless it appears that the witness' absence was procured by a party
>>
>> or (C) The witness is sick or imprisoned
>>
>> or (D) A party offering the deposition is unable to procure attendance of the witness by subpoena
>>
>> or (E) It is "in the interest of justice" *(upon application and notice)*
>
> (4) If only part of the deposition is used as evidence, an adverse party may require the remainder to be shown for fairness.
>
> 5. If a deposition is to be used against a party, the part must:
>> a. Be present at time of the deposition
>>
>> or b. Have reasonable notice of the deposition
>
> 6. A party may use depositions properly taken for another action involving the same subject.
>
> 7. Depositions taken without leave of court <u>cannot</u> be used if:
>> a. A party, with *due diligence*, is unable to obtain counsel at the deposition.
>>
>> or b. A party, with *greater than* <u>11 days</u> notice of the deposition, promptly moved for a protective order.

**(b) Objections to Admissibility** - may be made at any time during the trial or hearing.

**(c) Forms of Presentation**
    1. Depositions may be given in stenographic or non-stenographic form, unless the court rules otherwise.
    2. If non-stenographic, the party shall provide a transcript to the court.

**(d) Effect of Errors in Depositions**

    (1) <u>Notice</u> - All errors shall be deemed waived unless written objection is served promptly after the party gave notice.

    (2) <u>Disqualification of an Officer</u> - waived unless:
        a. An objection is made before the deposition
        b. An objection is made promptly after learning of the officer's disqualification

    (3) <u>Taking of Deposition</u>
        (A) *Competency of witness, relevancy, materiality of testimony* - not waived unless the objection would have definitely caused the deposition to be removed.
        (B) *Irregularities, manner of posing questions, oath affirmation, and conduct* - waived if not made promptly <u>at</u> the deposition.
        (C) *Objections to form of written questions* – waived unless objected to within <u>5 days</u> after the date that the last authorized questions were served.

    (4) <u>Completion/Return of Deposition</u>, *transcribed, certified, filed* - waived unless a motion to suppress is made within *reasonable time* (from when *due diligence* would have discovered it).

# RULE 33: Interrogatories To Parties

**(a) Availability**

1. Interrogatories may be served to any party once service of process is properly made.
2. A party may not serve more than 25 interrogatories
3. Leave of court is needed if:
   a. A party wants to serve more 25 interrogatories
   or b. A party wants to serve interrogatories early

**(b) Answers and Objections**

(1) <u>Answering Interrogatories</u>:
   a. Each question, unless it is objected to, must be answered:
      1. Separately
      2. Fully
      3. In Writing
      4. Under Oath
   b. If questions are objected to, the objecting party shall state the reasons for the objection and answer those questions that are not objectionable.
(2) <u>Signatures</u>:
   a. Answers - must be signed by the person writing them
   b. Objections - must be signed by the attorney making them
(3) <u>Time Limitation</u>:
   a. Must return interrogatories within <u>30 Days</u> after they were served.
   b. The court may change this time limitation, or parties may agree to new limits.
(4) <u>Objections</u>:
   a. Grounds for objections must be stated with specificity.
   b. Any objection not *timely* stated is waived unless good cause is shown.
(5) The party submitting interrogatories may move for a Rule 37(a) order for sanctions with respect to any objection or failure to answer an interrogatory.

**(c) Use at Trial**
 1. This rule is subject to Rule 26(b) and the Federal Rules of Evidence.
 2. A court may order that an interrogatory not be answered until certain discovery has been completed.

**(d) Option to Produce Business Records** - The answering party may opt to allow a questioning party to see records and get an answer himself (thus shifting the burden and time of research, auditing, etc. to his opponent).

# RULE 34:  Production of Documents and Entry For Inspection

**(a) Scope** - A party may request another party to:
 1. Produce any document or, information, in its custody (within the scope of Rule 26(b)).
 2. Permit entry (upon notice) for inspection and surveying (within the scope of Rule 26(b)).

**(b) Procedure**
 1. Requirements For the Request:
   a. Must state each item or category of items (must be stated separately)
   b. Must specify items to be inspected with *"reasonable particularity"*
   c. Must describe the manner in which the inspection will be done
   d. Must request a reasonable time and place for inspection
 2. Leave of court is needed to serve requests early.
 3. Within 30 Days (subject to change by agreement or by the court) of the request, the party (upon whom the request was served) shall state which items are permitted and which are objected to (and reasons for any objections).

**(c) Non-Parties** - may be compelled to produce documents under Rule 45.

# RULE 35: Physical/Mental Examinations

**(a) Order of Examination**
1. <u>Procedure</u>:
   a. Obtain a court order (by motion)
   b. Show *good cause* for the physical or mental examination
   c. Show that it is a *<u>material matter in controversy</u>*
2. Must give notice to all parties, specifying the:
   a. Examiner
   b. Time and place of exam
   c. Scope of examination

**(b) Report of Examiner**
(1) An Adverse party may request a report of the examination
(2) By requesting a report or taking an examiner's testimony, the examined party waives the privilege to get another examiner to testify for her.
(3) Agreements by parties may be made to alter these rules.

# RULE 36:  Request for Admission

**(a) Request for Admission**
1. A party may serve upon any other party a written request for an admission (for the pending action only) regarding statements of opinion or fact, the applicability of law to fact, and the truth of opinions, authenticity of documents, etc. (within the scope of Rule 26(b))
2. If no answer or objection is received within <u>30 Days</u> (can be changed by agreement of the parties or by the court) of the request for admission, a party is considered to admit the allegation.
3. If an objection is made, the reasons shall be stated in detail.
4. Admissions and denials must be specific to the related questions.

5. A party may not give "lack of knowledge and information" as a reason for not answering a request, unless:
    a. The party has made a reasonable inquiry
and b. There is not enough information to enable the party to admit or deny.
6. If court does not like an objection, it can order that an answer be made (and if it is not made, the court presumes an admission).
7. Leave of court is needed for early requests.

**(b) Effect of Admission**
1. Any admissions are *conclusively established*, unless the court grants a motion to <u>withdraw</u> or <u>amend</u> the admission.
2. Admissions are made only in regard to the pending action (i.e. cannot be used in other actions).
3. Amendments or withdrawals may be permitted on a showing that the *"presentation of the merits of the action will be subserved"* and if the opposing party cannot show that he will be prejudiced.

# RULE 37: Sanctions for Failure to Cooperate in Discovery

**(a) Motion for Order Compelling Disclosure of Discovery**

(1) <u>Appropriate Court</u>:
    a. *Where action pending* - motion required where deponent is a party
    b. *Where deposition is pending* - motion required if deponent is not a party
(2) <u>Motion</u>:
    (A) If a party fails to disclose (under 26(a)), the court may grant a <u>motion to compel disclosure</u>, upon showing a *good faith* effort to obtain the discovery without the court's help.
    (B) If a deponent refuses to answer, a party may make a motion for an <u>order compelling an answer</u>. If the court denies the motion, the deponent may be granted a <u>protective order</u> (under Rule 26(c)).
(3) <u>Evasive or Incomplete Answer</u> - considered a failure to answer.

(4) Expenses And Sanctions:
    a. If the motion is **granted**, or disclosure is made after the motion is filed, the party/deponent must pay reasonable fees spent to make the motion.
    b. If the motion is **denied**, and the motion is not *substantially justified*, the party making the motion must pay reasonable fees spent to oppose the motion.
    c. If the motion is denied in part and granted in part, expenses may be reasonably apportioned.
    d. All sanctions will be determined by a court hearing.

## (b) Failure to Comply With Order

(1) Sanctions By Court In District Where Deposition Is Taken - Failure to be sworn or provide an answer is considered contempt in that court.
(2) Sanctions By Court In District Where Action Is Pending - the Court may:
    (A) Conclude that matters sought to be discovered by a party are to be found in that party's favor
    (B) Refuse to allow the disobedient party to support or oppose designated claims or defenses
    (C) Render a default judgment or strike a pleading
    (D) Hold the disobedient person in contempt of court (unless it is in regards to a Rule 35 examination)
    (E) Require the opposing party to pay reasonable attorney's fees resulting from his disobedience, *unless* the court finds the disobedience *substantially justified.*

## (c) Failure to Disclose

(1) Penalty for a party that does not disclose information (i.e. information required under Rule 26(a)):
    a. The non-disclosing party shall not be allowed to use the undisclosed information as evidence at trial or at a hearing.
    b. Sanctions may be imposed if:
        1. There is no *substantial justification* not to disclose the information
    and 2. The failure to disclose was harmful
    c. The court may also impose other sanctions, including:
        1. Payment of reasonable expenses and/or attorneys' fees caused by the failure

2. Any action authorized under Rule 37(b)(2)(A), (B), and (C) (e.g. strike pleadings)
3. Informing the jury of the failure to disclose.

(2) If a party refuses to admit to the authenticity of a document and another party proves its authenticity, the court may impose fees spent to prove the document's validity, *unless:*

    (A) The request was objectionable under Rule 36(a)

or (B) The admission sought was of no substantial importance

or (C) The party failing to admit had reasonable grounds to believe that he would prevail on that matter

or (D) Other good cause is shown

**(d) Failure to Attend a Deposition, Serve Answers, or Respond to Production Requests** - subjects a party to Rule 37(b) sanctions.

**(e) Subpoena of a Person in a Foreign Country** - Abrogated

**(f) Expenses Against the United States** - Repealed

**(g) Failure to Participate in Framing a Discovery Plan** - If a *good faith* effort is made to agree on a 26(f) plan, reasonable attorneys fees to bring the plan to court will be imposed.

# VI. TRIALS

## RULE 38:  Right to a Jury Trial

**(a) Preserved Right** - The rights of a jury trial guaranteed by the 7th Amendment of the Constitution shall be preserved to parties "_inviolate_."

**(b) Demand** - Any party may demand a jury trial on any issue protected by the Constitution or a U.S. statute, by:
  (1) Serving a written "demand" on other parties
  and (2) Filing the demand (pursuant to Rule 5) no later than <u>10 Days</u> from service of the last pleading directed to such issue.

**(c) Specification of Issues**:
  1. In the demand, the party may specify which issues it wants to be tried by a jury. Otherwise, trial by jury is assumed to be demanded for all issues.
  2. If a party specifies only some issues, then the other party has <u>10 days</u> (unless the court shortens) to serve a "demand" for other issues he wishes to be tried by a jury.

**(d) Waiver**
  1. Failure to serve and file (pursuant to this rule) constitutes a waiver of the right to a jury.
  2. Once a demand is made, it may only be withdrawn if <u>both parties consent</u>.

**(e) Admiralty Claims** - These rules do not apply.

# RULE 39: Trial by Jury or Court

**(a) By Jury** - When a jury trial is demanded, the trial shall proceed as a jury action *unless:*
>> (1) The parties both consent on record (either in writing or on oral record in a hearing).
>> or (2) Upon motion or the court's own initiative, the court finds that a right to a jury trial on all or some of the issues does not exist under the Constitution or any U.S. statute (ex: the issue arises out of equity).

**(b) By Court**
> 1. If no jury demand is made, the case shall be tried by the court.
> 2. If a party neglects to make a "demand," the court (upon motion) has *discretion* to allow a jury trial, if it finds that such a demand might have been made *as of right.*

**(c) Advisory Jury and Trial By Consent**
> 1. For actions not triable as of right by jury, the court may try an issue with an *advisory jury* (by motion or on its own initiative).
> 2. In actions against the U.S. in which a statute provides for trial *without* a jury, a court may only use a jury if both parties agree.

# Rule 40: Assignment of Cases for Trial

> a. The district court shall provide, by local rule, the method of placing actions on the trial calendar:
>> (1) Without the request of the parties
>> or (2) Upon request of a party and notice to the other party
>> or (3) In such other manner as the courts deem expedient

> b. Precedence shall be given to actions given priority by a U.S. statute

# RULE 41: Dismissal Of Actions

**(a) Voluntary Dismissal**:
   (1) <u>By Plaintiff or Stipulation</u>:
      a. An action may be dismissed by the $\pi$ without a court order by:
         (i) filing a notice of dismissal at any time before service of an <u>answer</u> or <u>motion for summary judgment</u> is made (whichever is <u>sooner</u>)
      or (ii) filing a stipulation of dismissal singed by all parties who have appeared in the action
      b. Dismissal shall be <u>without prejudice</u>, unless:
         1. Otherwise stated in the notice
         2. The notice of dismissal operates as an adjudication upon the merits
         3. The case is filed by a $\pi$ who has already dismissed the action for the same claim in another court
      c. This subsection is subject to Rule 23(e), Rule 66, and any other U.S. statute.
   (2) <u>By Order of Court</u>:
      a. Unless dismissed under 41(a)(1), an action shall only be dismissed upon a court order.
      b. If a counterclaim has been pleaded by the Defendant prior to service of the $\pi$'s notice of dismissal then:
         1. The case cannot be dismissed if the counterclaim cannot remain as an independent action.
         2. $\pi$'s claim can be dismissed if the counterclaim can remain as an independent action.
      c. Dismissal of 41(a)(2) actions is <u>without prejudice</u>.

**(b) Involuntary Dismissal**:
   1. Defendant may move for a dismissal of any claim if $\pi$:
      a. Fails to prosecute
      or b. Fails to comply with the Federal Rules of Civil Procedure
      or c. Fails to comply with any court order

2. Dismissal under 41(b) is <u>with prejudice</u>, unless the court:
      a. States otherwise
    or b. Dismissed the case for <u>lack of jurisdiction</u>
    or c. Dismissed the case for <u>improper venue</u>
    or d. Dismissed the case for <u>failure to join a party</u> (pursuant to Rule 19)

**(c) Dismissal of Counterclaims**
    1. This rule applies to any claims, including:
      a. Counterclaims
    and b. Cross-claims
    and c. Third party claims
    2. If a voluntary dismissal is made by the claimant alone (pursuant to 41(a)(1)), it must be made:
      a. Before responsive pleadings are served
      b. Before introduction of evidence (at trial or hearing), if there are no responsive pleadings

**(d) Costs of Previously Dismissed Actions** - If π previously dismissed an action and is now reinstating it (i.e. bringing an action based on or including the <u>same</u> claim against the <u>same</u> Defendant), the court may impose costs for the previously dismissed action.

# RULE 42: Separate Trials; Consolidation

**(a) Consolidation of Cases** - If cases involve a <u>common question of law or fact,</u> a court may:
    1. Order:
      a. A joint hearing or trial of any issue in the action
    or b. A complete consolidation of the actions
    and 2. May make orders regarding the proceedings to avoid costs/delay

**(b) Separate Trials** - A court may split any claims for any of the following reasons:
    1. To avoid prejudice
    2. To further convenience
    3. To increase economic efficiency

# RULE 43: Taking Testimony

**(a) Form** - In all trials, the testimony of witnesses shall be taken orally in open court (unless otherwise provided in the Federal Rules of Evidence, these rules, or another U.S. statute).

**(b) Scope of Examination and Cross-Examination** - Abrogated

**(c) Record of Excluded Evidence** - Abrogated

**(d) Affirmation in Lieu of Oath** - Whenever an oath is required by these rules, a solemn <u>affirmation</u> may be accepted instead.

**(e) Evidence on Motions** - When a motion is based on facts not appearing on the record:
>    1. The court may hear the matter on affidavits presented by the parties.
> or 2. The court may direct the matter to be heard (wholly or partly) with oral testimony or depositions.

**(f) Interpreters**
>    1. The court may appoint an interpreter and fix its compensation.
>    2. The compensation, at the courts discretion:
>       a. Shall be paid out of funds provided by law
>    or b. Shall be paid by one or more of the parties (as the court directs)
>    or c. May be taxed as a cost of the litigation

# RULE 44: Proof of Official Record

**(a) Authentication**
>    (1) <u>Domestic Records</u> - Authentication of any records filed in the U.S. may be made by:
>       a. An official publication
>    or b. A copy signed by an officer (or the officer's deputy)
>          1. The officer must have *legal custody* of the actual record
>          2. The copy must be accompanied by a certificate stating that such officer has custody
>          3. <u>The accompanying certificate may be made by</u>:

> a. The judge of the court or jurisdiction where the record is filed.
>
> or b. Any public officer having a "seal of office" and official duties in the jurisdiction where the record is kept

(2) <u>Foreign Records</u> - May be authenticated by:
>  a. An official publication
>  or b. A signed copy of record which is:
>> 1. Signed by a person authorized to make the attestation
>> and 2. Accompanied by a certificate as to them genuineness of the officer's signature and the position of:
>>> (i) The attesting person
>>> or (ii) Any foreign official whose signature or position relates to the attestation

>  c. <u>Final Certification</u>
>> 1. A final certification may be made by a secretary of an embassy or other U.S. agent in the foreign country.
>> 2. After reasonable time is given for all parties to investigate the authenticity of the documents, the court may:
>>> (i) Admit an attested copy without final certification
>>> or (ii) Allow the foreign official record to be evidenced by an attested summary, with or without final certification
>> 3. Final certification is not necessary if the record and attestation are certified pursuant to a treaty or agreement with that country.

**(b) Lack of Record** - To prove that a record does not exist, or has not been recorded, a party must:
> 1. Provide a written statement that no record was found after a *diligent search*
> 2. Have the statement authenticated by the appropriate authority, pursuant to Rules 44(a)(1) and 44(b)(2) (above).

**(c) Other Proof** - *Any other method of proving the existence of a record or the lack of a record may be permitted if authorized by law.*

# RULE 44.1: Determination of Foreign Law

1. A party intending to raise a question involving foreign law must give notice of his intention in *either*:
   a. The pleadings
   or b. A *reasonable* written notice
2. In determining foreign law, a court may consider any relevant sources and testimony (admissible under the Federal Rules of Evidence).
3. The court's determination on foreign law shall be treated as a **ruling on a question of law.**

# RULE 45: Subpoena

**(a) Form; Issuance**
  (1) Requirements for a Valid Subpoena:
    (A) The subpoena must state the name of the court from which it is issued
    (B) The subpoena must state:
      1. The title of the action
      2. The name of the court in which the action is pending
      3. The action's civil action number
    (C) The subpoena must command each person to:
      1. Attend and give testimony
      or 2. Produce or permit copying and inspection of designated documents or other tangible possessions in their custody
      or 3. Permit inspection of premises at a specified time and place
    Note: A command to produce evidence or to permit inspection may be joined with a command to appear at trial, hearing or deposition, or may be issued separately.
    (D) The subpoena must set forth the text of Rules 45(c) and 45(d).
  (2) Court Issuing Subpoena:
    a. **Subpoena to Attend Trial**: Must be issued in the court in which trial is to be held.
    b. **Subpoena for Discovery:** Must be issued by the court in the district where discovery is to be made (ex: deposition, inspection, etc.).

(3) <u>Person Issuing Subpoena</u>:
      a. The clerk shall sign a blank subpoena form, which the party must complete before serving.
      b. An attorney, as an officer of the court, may also sign and issue a subpoena on behalf of a court in which the attorney is authorized to practice.

## (b) Serving the Subpoena

(1) <u>Method of Service</u>:
      a. Server must be over 18 years.
      b. Server must be a non-party.
      c. Method of service:
         1. By delivering a copy to the intended person
    and 2. Giving the person to attend travel expenses, if:
         a. Attendance is commanded
      and b. The subpoena is not brought on behalf of the U.S.
    and 3. If the subpoena is for production or inspection, prior notice shall be served on each party (pursuant to 5(b)).

(2) <u>Territorial Limits of Subpoena</u> - The subpoena may be served:
      a. Within the district of the court from which it is issued
      b. Outside the district if it is within <u>100 miles</u> of the trial, deposition, or inspection specified in the subpoena.
      c. Anywhere in the state of the trial and discovery, where that state's courts or statutes permit.

(3) <u>Proof of Service</u> - Shall be made by filing the following with the clerk of the court in which the subpoena is issued:
      a. A <u>statement</u> of the date and manner of service
    and b. The <u>names</u> of the persons served
    and c. A <u>certification</u> by the person who made service

## (c) Protection of Persons Subject to Subpoenas

(1) A party responsible for issuing a subpoena must take *reasonable steps* to avoid imposing *undue burden or expense* on the person subject to the subpoena. (The court may enforce this duty with sanctions, such as lost earnings and reasonable attorney's fees)

(2) **Production and Inspection:**
    (A) <u>Appearances:</u>
        A person commanded to produce discovery or to permit inspection need not appear in person, unless they are also commanded to appear for a:
           1. Deposition
        or 2. Hearing
        or 3. Trial
    (B) <u>Objections:</u>
        1. Within <u>14 days</u> of service of the subpoena, the party subject to production or inspection may serve a *written objection* upon the other party or his attorney.
        2. Once an objection is made, a party may not obtain production or inspection without a court order.
        3. The person who originally served the subpoena may make a **motion to compel production,** upon notice to the objecting party.

(3) **Modification**
    (A) Upon a *timely* motion, the issuing court may modify or quash a subpoena for any of the following reasons:
        (i) It fails to allow *reasonable time* for compliance
        or (ii) It requires a person who is not a party or officer to a party to travel more than 100 miles from his home or place of business for anything except attending trial
        or (iii) It requires disclosure of privileges or other protected matter, and no exceptions or waivers apply
        or (iv) It subjects a person to *undo burden*

    (B) <u>Modification and Condition</u>
        1. The court may quash or modify a subpoena to protect a person affected by it or subject to it if it:
           (i) Requires disclosure of a trade secret or other confidential commercial information
           or (ii) Requires disclosure of an unretained expert's opinion or information not directly relating to the dispute
           or (iii) Requires a non-party to travel more than 100 miles to attend a trial

2. The court may order appearance or production only upon *specific conditions* if:
   a. *Either:*
      i. A substantial need for the testimony or material is shown.
      or ii. Discovery cannot be otherwise met without undue hardship.
   and b. The party assures that the person to whom the subpoena is addressed will be *reasonably compensated.*
   and c. The subpoena *either*:
      (i) Requires disclosure of a trade secret or other commercial information
      or (ii) Requires disclosure of *either:*
         a. An unretained expert's opinion
         or b. Information not directly relating to the suit
      or (iii) Requires a non-party to travel more than 100 miles to attend trial.

## (d) Duties in Responding to Subpoena

(1) A person responding to a subpoena to produce documents must produce them in an organized manner:
   a. As kept in the *usual course of business*
   or b. Labeled to correspond with the categories in the demand
(2) When information subject to the subpoena is withheld because the producing party deems it privileged, the producing party must:
   a. Specify the nature of the documents
   and b. Expressly state why the information is being withheld
   and c. Be specific enough to allow the demanding party to contest the claim

## (e) Contempt - Failure to obey a served subpoena will result in contempt of the court in which the subpoena is issued, unless an *adequate excuse* is made (ex: a non-party is required to travel more than 100 miles).

# RULE 46: Exceptions Unnecessary

1. Formal exceptions to rulings are only necessary where specified.
2. When required, notice of objection may be made at the time the ruling or order of the court is made or sought, by making known to the court:
     a. The action the party desires the court to take
  and b. The party's objections to the court's actions, and the reasons for them
3. The absence of an objection to a ruling does not prejudice a party if he had no opportunity to object to it at the time it was made.

# *VII. JURY AND TRIAL RULES*

## RULE 47: Selection of Jurors

**(a) Examination of Jurors**
    1. The court may permit parties (or their attorneys) to examine prospective jurors (or the court may itself do so).
    2. If the court examines the jurors, it shall permit the parties *("as it deems proper")* to *either*:
        a. Supplement the examination with further inquiry
     or b. Submit to the prospective jurors additional questions prepared by the parties.

**(b) Peremptory Challenges** - The court shall allow peremptory challenges of jurors (pursuant to 28 USC §1870).

**(c) Excuse** - The court may, for good cause, excuse a juror from service during trial or deliberation.

## RULE 48: Number of Jurors

    a. The court shall have between 6 and 12 jurors.
    b. All jurors must participate in the verdict, unless excused pursuant to Rule 47(c).
    c. Unless the parties otherwise agree,
        (1) The verdict shall be unanimous.
     and (2) No verdict shall be taken from a jury reduced to *less than* 6 people.

# RULE 49: Special Verdicts and Interrogatories

**(a) Special Verdicts** - The court may require a jury to return only a
**special verdict.**
>    1. The special verdict must be in the form of a special <u>written</u>
>       finding upon each issue of fact.
>    2. The court may submit to the jury:
>> a. Written questions susceptible of absolute or other brief
>>    answers
>> or b. Written forms of the several special findings which
>>    could properly be made from the evidence or pleadings
>> or c. Other methods of submitting issues (as it deems appropriate)
>    3. The court shall give the jury instructions as necessary to
>       facilitate a jury decision.
>    4. If the court omits any issue of fact for the jury to decide, the
>       parties must demand submission *before the jury retires*.
>    5. Those issues omitted may be decided by the court.

**(b) General Verdict**
>    1. The court may submit forms for a **general verdict** accompanied by
>       *written* interrogatories on issues of fact necessary to decide a
>       general verdict.
>    2. The court shall give appropriate instructions to help the jurors
>       make their decision.
>    3. When the general verdict and written answers are *"harmonious,"*
>       appropriate judgment shall be made.
>    4. <u>Inconsistencies:</u>
>> a. <u>When answers are consistent with each other, yet 1 or more
>>    answer is inconsistent with the general verdict</u>, the judge
>>    may:
>>> 1. Affirm jury's verdict
>>> or 2. Enter judgment in accordance with their answers (and not
>>>    the general verdict).
>>> or 3. Send the jury back for further considerations
>>> or 4. Order a new trial
>> b. <u>When answers are inconsistent with each other and inconsistent
>>    with the general verdict</u>, the judge shall:
>>> 1. Send the jury back for further considerations
>>> or 2. Order a new trial

*as appropriate*

# RULE 50: Judgments and Jury Trials:

**(a) Judgment as a Matter of Law** (JNOV; "Directed Verdict")

(1) The court may grant a motion for judgment as a matter of law, if, after being heard, there is no *legally sufficient evidentiary basis* for a *reasonable* jury to have found for a party on a certain issue (because it would be contrary to controlling law).

(2) Requirements for a Motion for Judgment as a Matter of Law

    a. Must be made _before_ the case is submitted to the jury

    b. Must specify the judgment sought

    c. Must state the applicable rule of law and its relationship to the facts

    d. Must be made _after_ the non-movant has been <u>fully heard</u>

**(b) Renewal for Judgment After Trial; Alternative Motion for New Trial**

1. <u>Renewal of Motion for Judgment after Trial</u>:

    a. If the original motion is denied, the court is deemed to have submitted the case to the jury.

    b. A jury verdict will be subject to a later determination of the legal questions raised by the motion.

    c. The motion may be "renewed" after the verdict by filing and serving it within <u>10 days</u> after *entry of judgment.*

2. <u>Alternative Motion for a New Trial</u> - May be requested in the *alternative* or *joined* with renewal of the motion (See Rule 50(c)).

3. <u>Judgment on the Renewed Motion</u>

    a. _If a Verdict is returned_, the court may:

        1. Allow the original judgment to stand

      or 2. Direct entry of judgment as a matter of law (reverse)

      or 3. Order a new trial

    b. _If No Verdict Returned_, the court may:

        1. Direct entry of judgment as a matter of law

      or 2. Order a new trial

## (c) Conditions of Granting Judgment as a Matter of Law

(1) If a motion for judgment is granted, the court must also rule on a <u>motion for a new trial</u> (if it was made) as follows:

- The Court must decide whether a new trial should be granted if the judgment is vacated or reversed after the JNOV

- The court must describe specific grounds for granting or denying the motion for retrial.

- Even if the motion for a new trial is conditionally granted (i.e. if the JNOV is later vacated or reversed), the judgment is still final. If the JNOV is later reversed on appeal, the new trial goes forward (unless the appellate court ordered otherwise).

- If the motion for retrial is denied, the denial may be appealed. If the JNOV is later reversed on appeal, the appellate court determines what subsequent proceedings take place.

(2) If judgment as a matter of law has been rendered against a party, that party may serve a motion for a new trial (under Rule 59) no later than <u>10 days</u> after the judgment was entered.

## (d) Denial of a Motion for Judgment as a Matter of Law

1. The successful party may, on appeal, request a new trial, if: the motion was *denied*, and the appellate court finds that the <u>trial court erred</u> in denying the motion for judgment.

2. If the <u>appellate court reverses</u> the trial court's judgment it may also find that:

    a. The appellee is entitled to a new trial

    or b. The trial court shall determine if a new trial should be granted

# RULE 51: Instructions to Jury

1. At the close of evidence (or at such earlier time as the court allows) any party may file a written request for the court to instruct the jury on a certain law.
2. Prior to their arguments to the jury, the court shall inform counsel of its proposed action based on their requests.
3. The court may instruct the jury before or after the arguments, or both.
4. Objections to giving or failure to give jury instructions must be made *before* the jury retires to consider its verdict.
5. Objections must specifically state the grounds for objection.

# RULE 52: Findings By The Court

**(a) Effect**
1. Scope: This rule applies to actions tried without a jury or with an advisory jury.
2. The court shall state *separately* its conclusions of law and its findings of fact.
3. Judgment shall be entered pursuant to Rule 58.
4. In granting or refusing interlocutory injunctions, the court must also specifically state findings of facts and law as grounds for its conclusion.
5. Review of Facts (on appeal); Standard of Review:
    a. The findings of fact shall only be set aside if they are *clearly erroneous*.
    b. *Due regard* must be given to the trial judge's opportunity to determine a witnesses' credibility.
6. Findings of a master shall be considered findings of the court.
7. Findings of fact may be stated orally (and recorded) or written in an opinion or memorandum.
8. Findings of fact and conclusions of law are not needed for motions under Rule 12 or Rule 56.

**(b) Amendment**
1. <u>Motion to Amend</u>:
   - a. A motion for amendment may be made within <u>10 Days</u> after entry of judgment.
   - b. The motion may be made along with a motion for a new trial (pursuant to Rule 59).
2. The court may amend its findings or make additional findings, and change the judgment accordingly.
3. When findings of fact are made by the court, a party may raise a question of <u>sufficiency of the evidence</u>, *without:*
   - a. Making a motion to amend
   - b. Making a motion for judgment
   - c. Raising objections to such findings in the district court

**(c) Judgment on Partial Findings** ("Mini-trial" or "Partial Judgment")
1. <u>Scope</u>: This subsection applies to trials heard <u>without a jury</u>.
2. A judge may enter judgment as a matter of law *before* all the evidence is heard if:
   - a. A party has been <u>fully heard</u> on certain issues
   - and b. The claim or defense is controlled by the issues
   - and c. The only way the case could be won is if one particular issue was found in favor of that party
   - and d. The court did not find the issue in favor of that party
3. The court may also wait until the close of all the evidence to make its decision.
4. The court shall support its decision as required by Rule 52(a).

# RULE 53: Masters

## (a) Appointment and Compensation

1. A "Master" includes:
   a. A Referee
   b. An Auditor
   c. An Examiner
   d. An Assessor
2. The judge may appoint a special master to any action pending in its court.
3. Compensation:
   a. Compensation for the master shall be fixed by the court.
   b. Payment shall be made from the parties or a specified fund.
   c. No compensation is made if the master is a U.S. magistrate judge.
   d. A master cannot hold his report as security; rather, if he is not paid by the parties, he may obtain a <u>writ of execution</u> to obtain payment.

## (b) Reference

1. Reference to a Master's report shall be *"the exception and not the rule."*
2. <u>Master reports with jury trials</u> - The court shall use the master's report only if issues are *complicated.*
3. <u>Master reports with non-jury trials</u> - The court shall make reference to master's report only in the following situations:
   a. If there is a showing that some *exceptional condition* requires it.
   or b. In matters involving an accounting.
   or c. In matters involving a difficult computation of damages.
4. Upon consent of the parties, a magistrate may be used as a special master; The magistrate is not subject to the limitations in Rule 53(b).

### (c) Powers

1. The "<u>Order of Reference</u>" orders the appointment of the Master.
2. <u>The Order of Reference</u> may:
    a. Specify or limit the Master's powers
    b. Direct the master to report only upon particular issues
    c. Direct the master to do or perform particular acts
    d. Direct the master to receive and report evidence only
    e. Fix the time and place for the hearings period
    f. Fix the time and place for the master to file his report
3. <u>The Master's Powers</u>:
    a. He shall *"do all acts and take all measures necessary or proper for the efficient performance of his duties."*
    b. He shall regulate all proceedings in every hearing before him.
    c. He may require production of evidence for any matter described in the order of reference.
    d. He may rule upon the admissibility of evidence (subject to authority in the order of reference).
    e. He may call witnesses and examine parties under oath
4. Upon request of the parties, the master shall record evidence as provided by the Federal Rules of Evidence for non-jury trials.

### (d) Proceedings

*(1) Meetings*
    a. After an order of reference is made, the court shall give the master a copy of the order.
    b. Upon receipt, the master must arrange for a time and place of a first meeting, which must be held within <u>20 Days</u> after the order was issued.
    c. The master must notify the parties of the initial meeting.
    d. It is the duty of the master to proceed with *"all reasonable diligence."*
    e. Either party may apply to the court to speed up the master's proceeding (upon notice to the parties and the master)
    f. If a party does not show up at a hearing, the master may *either*:
        1. Proceed *ex-parte*
        or 2. Re-schedule the hearing for a further date (and notify the parties of the new schedule)

*(2) Witnesses*
>    a. Parties may procure the attendance of witnesses by subpoena (under Rule 45).
>    b. If a witness fails to attend without a valid excuse, he may be held in contempt of court and punished pursuant to Rule 37 and Rule 45.

*(3) Statement of Accounts*
>    a. When an action involves an accounting, the master can specify the form in which the accounting statements may be submitted.
>    b. The master can also require a statement by a CPA (to determine the validity of the statements).
>    c. If a party objects to a particular accounting statement or item on that statement, the master may:
>>        1. Require a different form of the statement to be furnished
>>        2. Require that the statements or items in the objection be proved by:
>>>            a. Oral examination
>>>            or b. Interrogatories
>>>            or c. Other manners as the master directs

## (e) Report

*(1) Contents and Filing*
>    a. The master must prepare a report upon all matters submitted to him in the order of reference.
>    b. If the master was required to make a finding of fact or conclusion of law, he shall describe his conclusions in the report.
>    c. The master shall:
>>        1. File his report with the court
>>        and 2. Serve:
>>>            a. A notice to all parties that he filed his report
>>>            b. A copy of his report to all parties
>    d. If the trial is without a jury, the master must also file a transcript of the proceedings, evidence and exhibits (unless otherwise indicated in the order of reference).

*(2) Non-Jury Actions*

    a. The court must accept the master's findings of fact unless they are *clearly erroneous.*

    b. A party may serve written objections to the master's report within <u>10 Days</u> of the notice of filing.

    c. Objections to the report and motions directed to the report must be made as prescribed in Rule 6(d).

    d. After hearing objections, the Court may do any of the following:

        1. Adopt the report

        2. Modify the report

        3. Reject the report (in whole or in part)

        4. Receive further evidence

        5. Recommit the case to the master with instructions

*(3) Jury Actions*

    a. The master is not required to report the *evidence.*

    b. The master's findings are only admissible as evidence that may be read to the jury (subject to objections).

*(4) Stipulation As To Findings*

    a. The effect of a master's report is the same whether or not both parties agreed to defer the issues to the master.

    b. The master's **findings of fact**, however, are only final when the parties agree that the master's findings shall be final.

    c. Only **questions of law** arising from the report can be considered after the parties' agreement.

*(5) Draft Report* - Before submitting his official report, a master may submit a draft report to the parties in order to obtain their suggestions.

**(f) Application to Magistrate Judges** - Rule 53 only applies to magistrate judges if the order referring a matter to him expressly subjects the him to this rule.

# VIII. JUDGMENT

## RULE 54: Judgments; Costs

**(a) "Judgment"**
1. "Judgment" refers to any *appealable* order or decree.
2. A judgment shall not contain any of the following:
   - a. A recital of the pleadings
   - or b. The report of a master
   - or c. The record of prior proceedings

**(b) Judgments Upon Multiple Claims or Parties**
1. The judge may <u>direct an entry</u> of a **final judgment** for some (but not all) of the issues involved.
2. <u>Requirements for a Directed Entry</u>:
   - a. The Judge must make an "<u>Express Determination</u>" that there is no *just* reason to delay judgment <u>on an issue</u>.
   - and b. The entry of judgment must be upon an "<u>express direction</u>," specifically directed to the issue being adjudicated early.
3. If the above requirements are not met, any order or decision adjudicating less than all of the issues or all of the parties involved shall:
   - a. <u>Not</u> terminate the action as to any claims or parties (i.e. the decision is not a final judgment, and, therefore, not immediately appealable).
   - b. Be subject to revision before final judgment on the entire action is entered.

**(c) Demand for Judgment**
1. <u>Judgments by Default</u>: A default judgment cannot exceed (or differ from) what was requested in the pleadings.
2. <u>Judgment without Default</u>: Judgments not reached by default may be different from or exceed that which was demanded in the pleadings.

**(d) Costs**

(1) <u>Costs Other Than Attorney Fees</u>:

    a. Costs may be allowed to the prevailing party *unless:*

        1. The court otherwise directs

    or 2. The rules or statute otherwise direct

    b. Costs imposed against a U.S. government agency or officer are limited to those which are "permitted by law."

    c. Costs may be taxed by the clerk on <u>1 day's</u> notice.

    d. In order to appeal costs, a motion must be served within <u>5 days</u> of the clerk's notice.

(2) <u>Attorney Fees</u>

    (A) Claims for attorney fees (and related non-taxable expenses) shall be made by motion, *unless* the substantive law governing the action provides that such fees are to be included in the damages.

    (B) <u>Motion to Recover Attorney Fees</u>

        1. Must be made within <u>14 days</u> after entry of judgment, *unless* otherwise provided by statute or court order.

        2. <u>The motion must specify</u>:

            a. The judgment and the statute, rule, or other grounds entitling the movant to costs

         and b. The amount sought or a fair estimate of the amount sought

         and c. The terms of any agreement involving fees (if directed by the court)

    (C) <u>Adversary Submissions</u>

        1. Upon request of a party or class member, the court shall allow an opportunity for *adversary submissions* with respect to the motion to recover costs (pursuant to Rule 43(e) or Rule 78).

        2. The court may determine issues of liability (regarding which expenses qualify to be subject to liability) for fees before receiving submissions (i.e. the court may determine the appropriate amount potentially recoverable, but not whether or not there should be recovery).

        3. The court shall find the facts and state its conclusions of law (pursuant to Rule 52(a)).

        4. The judgment shall be set forth in a separate document, as provided in Rule 58.

(D) <u>Local Provisions</u>
    1. Local rules may be prescribed to establish special procedures to resolve issues relating to fees, without extensive evidentiary hearings.
    2. The court may refer issues involving the valuation of attorney fees to a Master (under Rule 53) or Magistrate (under Rules 72-75).

(e) The provisions of subparagraphs (A) through (D) do not apply to claims for fees and expenses resulting from **sanctions** for violating these rules.

# RULE 55: Default

**(a) Entry**: The Clerk shall enter default judgment when:
    1. A party has failed to plead (or otherwise defend itself as provided by the rules)
and  2. Affirmative relief is sought against the defaulting party
and  3. The fact that a party defrauded is proved by an affidavit or otherwise

**(b) Procedures for Default Judgment**

(1) <u>By The Clerk</u> - The clerk may enter default judgment if:
    a. π's claim is for a <u>sum certain</u> or computable amount
and b. <u>π files an affidavit</u> with the clerk requesting and attesting to the amount due
and c. The Defendant had defaulted for <u>failure to appear</u>
and d. The defaulting party is not an infant or incompetent

(2) <u>By The Court</u> - For all other cases, where the amount due is not certain:
    a. The party entitled to a judgment by default shall apply to the court for judgment.

b. If a party against whom a default judgment is rendered has already appeared, the defaulting party shall be served with a written notice of the application for default judgment, *at least* 3 days before the hearing for default judgment.

c. Default judgment cannot be made against infants or incompetents, *unless* they are represented in the action by a guardian or other representative who has appeared.

d. The court may conduct a hearing or order references before entering a default judgment, if it is necessary to:
>    1. Take an account or determine the amount of damages
> or 2. Establish the trust of any averment with evidence
> or 3. Make an investigation on any other matter

e. The court shall extend the right to a jury trial when any U.S. statute requires.

**(c) Setting Aside Default** - The court may set aside an entry for default judgment if:
>    1. Good cause is shown
> or 2. Cause under Rule 60(b) is shown

**(d) Parties Entitled to Default Judgment** –

1. Default Judgment applies to the following parties:
   a. Plaintiffs
   b. Third-Party Plaintiffs
   c. Parties pleading Cross-claims
   d. Parties pleading Counterclaims

2. Default Judgment is subject to Rule 54(c) limitations (i.e. it cannot exceed the demand for judgment).

**(e) Judgment Against the United States** - No default judgment shall be entered against the U.S. government, agency, or officer, unless the claimant established a claim of right to relief with evidence *satisfactory* to the court.

# RULE 56:  Summary Judgment

**(a) For Claimant (π):** A party may move for summary judgment (with or without supporting affidavits) *after* either:

    1. <u>20 days</u> from commencement of the action

or 2. Service of a motion for summary judgment ("SJ") by the adverse party

**(b) For Defendant:** May move for Summary Judgment at *any time* (with or without supporting affidavits).

**(c) Motions and Proceedings**

    1. A Motion for SJ must be served to the adverse party at least <u>10 days</u> before the scheduled hearings.

    2. The adverse party may serve opposing affidavits *at any time* before the hearing.

    3. Summary Judgment must be based upon:

        a. Pleadings

        b. Depositions

        c. Interrogatories

        d. Admissions

        e. Affidavits

    4. Summary Judgment shall be rendered if, based on the above:

        a. There is no *genuine issue of any material fact* shown (discretionary)

    and b. The moving party is entitled to judgment *as a matter of law.*

**(d) Case Not Fully Adjudicated on Motion**

    1. If only part of the case is adjudicated, the court shall determine which facts remain at issue for trial.

    2. The Judge shall file an order establishing the "<u>adjudicated facts</u>" and how they affect the amount in controversy.

**(e) Defending Motion for SJ:**
    1. <u>Requirements for Affidavits</u>:
        a. Must include personal knowledge of facts (admissible under the Federal Rules of Evidence)
        b. Shall show that the affiant is competent to testify
        c. The court may permit the affidavit to be supplemented by depositions, interrogatories, or other affidavits.

    2. <u>Responding to a Motion for SJ</u>:
        a. The adverse party must set forth *specific facts* showing that there is a genuine issue for trial (cannot rely on pleadings).
        b. If the adverse party cannot show that there is a genuine issue, SJ shall be entered against her *if appropriate* (given an opportunity for discovery).

**(f) When Affidavits are Unavailable**
    If a party opposing a motion for SJ can show in its affidavit that it cannot obtain affidavits containing facts <u>*essential*</u> to justify it's opposition to SJ, then the court may:
        1. Refuse the application for SJ
    or 2. Order a continuance to permit affidavits to be obtained (or other depositions or discovery to be had)
    or 3. Make such order as it deems just

**(g) Affidavits Made in Bad Faith** (to delay the proceeding)
    1. A party making an improper affidavit shall pay the other party's reasonable expenses (including attorney fees) associated with the motion for SJ.
    2. The offending party or attorney may be guilty of contempt.

# RULE 57: Declaratory Judgment

 a. The existence of another remedy does not preclude a judgment for declaratory relief in cases where it is appropriate.
 b. The procedure for obtaining a declaratory judgment pursuant to 28 USC §2201 shall be in accordance with these rules.
 c. The court may order a speedy hearing of an action for a declaratory judgment, and may advance it on the calendar.
 d. A jury trial may be demanded (subject to Rule 38 and 39).

# RULE 58: Entry Of Judgment

 (1) The clerk shall prepare, sign, and enter judgment (without waiting for the court's direction to do so), upon:
     a. The Court's Decision, if:
         1. The decision was made without a jury
      and 2. The decision *either:*
             i. Denies relief
          or ii. Awards a certain sum
      or b. The General Verdict
 (2) The Judge must first approve the clerk's form if judgment is entered upon:
     a. The court's decision (non-jury)
   or b. A special verdict
   or c. A general verdict with special interrogatories
 3. Each judgment shall be recorded on a separate document.
 4. There shall be no delays in entering orders to tax costs or award fees.
 5. Attorneys may provide the form of judgments (to be filed by the clerk) upon the judge's approval.
 6. Judgment entry must be done pursuant to Rule 79(a).

# RULE 59: New Trials and Judgment Amendments

**(a) Grounds** - A new trial may be granted on all or some of the issues in the following instances:

    (1) <u>Trial By Jury</u> - allowed for any reason courts have (until now) allowed a new trial (See Rule 60(b)).

    (2) <u>Trial Without a Jury</u> –

        a. Allowed for any reason the courts have (until now) allowed a rehearing.

        b. Upon motion for new trial, courts may:

            1. Open judgment (if one has been entered)

      or 2. Take additional testimony

      or 3. Amend a finding of fact

      or 4. Amend a finding/ conclusions of law

      or 5. Make new findings of fact or law

      or 6. Direct entry of a new judgment (or affirm the original judgment)

**(b) Time Limitation** - The motion must be served no later than <u>10 Days</u> after entry of judgment.

**(c) Serving Affidavits**

    1. When a motion for a new trial is based on affidavits, the affidavits shall be served <u>with the motion</u>.

    2. The opposing party has <u>10 Days</u> after service of the motion to serve opposing affidavits (may be extended to no more than <u>20 days</u> (total) if good cause is shown or the parties agree).

**(d) New Trial on Court's Initiative**

    1. The court may order a new trial on its own initiative, for any reason it may have granted a new trial by motion.

    2. The court may order a new trial for reasons not specified in the motion *after* giving <u>notice</u> and an <u>opportunity</u> to be heard.

    3. The court must specify the grounds for its decision

    4. The court must order a new trial no later than <u>10 days</u> after entry of judgment.

**(e) Motion to Alter or Amend Judgment** - Must be served no later than <u>10 Days</u> after entry of judgment.

# RULE 60: Relief From Judgment

**(a) Clerical Mistakes** in judgments, orders, or other parts of the record arising out of <u>oversight</u> or <u>omission</u>:

1. Such errors may be corrected by motion or on the court's initiative
2. Such errors may be corrected any time before an appeal is docketed
3. Once an appeal begins, leave of court is needed or a correction to be made.

## (b) Relief from Judgment

i. The court may relieve a party or its legal representative from a final judgment, order, or proceeding if:

   (1) There was mistake, inadvertence, surprise, or excusable neglect.

   or (2) Newly discovered evidence was found, which by *due diligence* could not have been discovered in time to move for a new trial.

   or (3) There was fraud, misrepresentation, or other misconduct of an adverse party

   or (4) The judgment is void (ex: jurisdiction is not appropriate).

   or (5) *Either:*

      a. The judgment was satisfied

      or b. The judgment has been released or discharged

      or c. A prior judgment, upon which the judgment is based, is reversed

      or d. It is no longer equitable that the judgment should have prospective application

   or (6) There exists any other reason justifying relief from the operation of the judgment.

ii. <u>Time to Make Motion</u>

1. "<u>Term Rule</u>": For reasons (1), (2), and (3), a motion must be made within <u>1 year</u> from when the judgment or order was entered.
2. For reasons (4), (5), and (6), a motion must be made within a *<u>reasonable time</u>* from when the judgment was entered or taken.

# RULE 61: Harmless Error

a. The following are not valid grounds for granting a new trial, setting aside a verdict, or otherwise altering a judgment, *unless* refusal to take such action appears to the court *inconsistent with substantial justice:*
  1. Error in admission or exclusion of evidence
  2. Error or defect in ruling or order in anything done or omitted by the court (or by any of the parties).
b. At every stage of the proceedings, the court must disregard any error or defect in the proceedings which does not affect the substantial rights of the parties.

# RULE 62: Stay of Proceedings to Enforce a Judgment

**(a) Automatic Stay**
  1. Except as otherwise stated below, there shall be an automatic stay of 10 days after the date that any judgment or decision is entered for execution.
  2. Unless the court orders otherwise, an interlocutory or final judgment shall not be stayed during the period after its entry, until the appeal is taken, for judgments involving:
      a. An injunction
      or b. A receivership
      or c. An order directing an accounting in an action for a patent infringement

**(b) Stay on Motion for New Trial or for Judgment**
  1. The court may stay the execution of any order or judgment proceeding to enforce it
      a. In the court's discretion
      b. For the security of the adverse party
  2. The stay may be extended, pending the disposition of:
      a. A motion for new trial
      or b. A motion to alter or amend a judgment (pursuant to Rule 59)
      or c. A motion for relief from a judgment or order (pursuant to Rule 60)
      or d. A motion for judgment or directed verdict (pursuant to Rule 50)

or e. A motion to amend or make additional findings (pursuant to Rule 52(b))

## (c) Injunction Pending Appeal

   i. On appeals from interlocutory or final judgments involving injunctions, the court, *in its discretion,* may <u>suspend</u>, <u>modify</u>, <u>grant</u> or <u>restore</u> an injunction during the pendency of the appeal, upon such terms as it considers proper for the security of the adverse party's rights.

   ii. No such order can be made in a district court created by a U.S. statute, with 3 judges, *unless:*

      (1) It is made by the court sitting in open court

   or (2) All 3 judges assent to and sign the order

## (d) Stay on Appeal

   1. The appellant may obtain a stay by giving court a <u>Supersedes Bond</u>.

   2. The Stay shall be subject to the exceptions in Rule 62(a).

   3. The bond may be given at or after the time of filing the notice of appeal.

   4. The Stay is effective when the Supersedes Bond is approved by the court.

## (e) Stay in Favor of the U.S. - No bond or security is needed from the U.S.

## (f) Stay According to State Law

A judgment debtor shall be accorded any <u>stay of execution</u> if the state where the property subject to a court lien is located would ordinarily entitle him to such a stay.

## (g) Power of the Appellate Court Not Limited

This rule does not limit the power of the appellate court to:

   a. Stay proceedings during pendency of an appeal

   or b. Suspend, modify, restore, or grant an injunction during the pendency of an appeal

   or c. Make any *appropriate* order to preserve the status-quo or the effectiveness of the judgment to be subsequently entered

**(h) Stay of Judgment with Multiple Claims or Parties**
When a court has ordered a final judgment pursuant to Rule 54(b), the court may:

    1. Stay enforcement of the judgment until the entering of a subsequent judgment

and 2. Prescribe such conditions as are necessary to secure satisfaction of a judgment to the party in whose favor it is entered.

# RULE 63: Inability of a Judge to Proceed

a. If a judge who has commenced a trial or hearing is unable to continue handling the case, any other judge may proceed with it upon:

    1. Certifying <u>familiarity</u> with the record

and 2. Determining that the proceedings may be completed <u>without prejudice</u> to the parties

b. In a hearing or trial without a jury, a party may request the recall of any witness, if:

    1. The witness' testimony is material and disputed

and 2. The witness is available to testify again, without undue burden

c. The successor judge may also recall any witness at her own initiative.

# RULE 64: Seizure of Person or Property

a. All remedies providing for seizure of person or property (in order to secure the satisfaction of an ultimate judgment) are available pursuant to the <u>state law</u> in which the district court presides.

b. <u>Rules Governing the Seizure</u>:

    (1) These rules governing seizure shall be subject to limitations by any U.S. statute.

    (2) Any such action must be <u>commenced</u> and <u>prosecuted</u> pursuant to these rules.

c. The remedies available under this section include:
  1. Arrest
 and 2. Attachment
 and 3. Garnishment
 and 4. Replevin
 and 5. Sequestration
 and 6. Other corresponding or equivalent remedies
d. These remedies are available whether or not:
  1. The remedy is ancillary to a state action
 or 2. The remedy must be obtained by an independent action

# RULE 65: Injunctions

## (a) Preliminary Injunction

(1) <u>Notice</u> - Notice to the adverse party must be given before a preliminary injunction may be issued.

(2) <u>Consolidation of Hearing with Trial on the Merits</u>

 a. Before or after hearings on an application for a preliminary injunction begin, the court may order that the trial itself be advanced and consolidated with the preliminary injunction hearing.

 b. Any evidence admitted during the preliminary injunction hearing will become part of the trial record (and therefore need not be repeated at trial).

 c. The court shall construe this subdivision so as to afford the parties any rights they may have to a jury trial.

## (b) Temporary Restraining Order

i. A Temporary Restraining Order ("TRO") may be granted <u>without notice</u> to the adverse party if:

 (1) It clearly appears from specific facts (in an affidavit or verified complaint), that *irreparable and immediate* injury, loss, or damage will result to the applicant before a hearing can be scheduled.

 and (2) The applicant's attorney certifies to the court in writing:
  a. Efforts made, if any, to give notice
  and b. Reasons why notice should not be required

  ii. <u>Every TRO granted without notice must</u>:
- a. Be endorsed with the date and hour of issuance
- b. Be filed with the clerk's office
- c. Be entered on the record
- d. Define the injury
- e. State why the injury is irreparable
- f. State why the order was granted without notice

  iii. <u>Duration of TROs issued without notice</u>:
- a. A TRO may not last longer than <u>10 Days</u>.
- b. A TRO time limit may be extended if:
  - 1. The adverse party consents to the extension
  - or 2. Within the initial 10 day period, the court extends the period for another <u>10 Days</u>, *for good cause shown.*
- c. Reasons for such an extension must be entered on the record.

  iv. <u>Motion for a Preliminary Injunction</u>
- a. When a TRO is granted without notice, the motion for a preliminary injunction shall be scheduled for a hearing at the *earliest possible time,* and takes precedence over all other matters (except for older matters of the same character).
- b. If the party requesting the TRO does not appear at the hearing to proceed with the application for a preliminary injunction, the court shall dissolve the TRO.
- c. The adverse party may appear and move to dissolve or modify the TRO with <u>2 Days</u> notice to the parties who obtained the TRO.
- d. If the adverse party moves to dissolve the TRO, the court shall proceed to decide the motion as *"expeditiously as the ends of justice require."*

## (c) Security

1. The applicant for a TRO or preliminary injunction must give security for the payment of any costs or damages incurred by the adverse party, if the TRO or preliminary injunction was wrongfully issued.
2. The court will determine the appropriate amount of security that the applicant must pay.
3. The U.S. government needs not post security to obtain a TRO or preliminary injunction.

**(d) Form and Scope of Injunction or Restraining Order**

    1. Any restraining order or grant of injunction shall:

        a. Include the <u>reasons for its issuance</u>, with specific terms

    and b. Describe the <u>acts to be restrained</u>, in reasonable detail

        (without reference to the complaint or other outside documents)

    2. The order is binding upon the following persons:

        a. The parties to the action

    and b. The parties' officers, agents, servants, employees, and attorneys

    and c. Those people in active concert or participation with the parties who also receive <u>actual notice</u> of the order.

**(e) Employer**

    1. These rules do not modify any U.S. statues relating to TROs or preliminary injunctions in the following actions:

        a. Actions affecting employers and employee

        b. Actions involving interpleader (pursuant to 28 USC 2361)

        c. Actions relating to 28 USC §2284, requiring (by act of Congress) a hearing by a district court of 3 judges.

# RULE 65.1: Security: Proceedings Against Sureties

    a. <u>Scope of Rule</u>: Rule 65.1 applies whenever these rules require the giving of a security payment, and security is given, in the form of a:

        1. Bond

    or 2. Stipulation

    or 3. Any other undertaking involving 1 or more sureties

    b. Each surety involved:

        1. Automatically submits itself to the jurisdiction of the court

    and 2. Irrevocably appoints the court clerk as the surety's agent upon whom papers may be served

    c. The surety's liability may be enforced on motion (i.e. There is no need for an independent action).

    d. Motions and notices affecting the surety may be served to the court clerk.

    e. The clerk must mail copies of the papers to the surety, if the address is known.

# RULE 66: Receivers Appointed By Federal Court

a. Actions in which <u>receivers</u> have been appointed can only be dismissed by a court order.

b. Actions involving receivers shall be governed by these rules, subject to local rules in the district courts.

# RULE 67: Deposit in Court

a. A party may deposit all or part of the relief sought, if:
    1. <u>The relief sought is a judgment of</u>:
        a. A sum of money (or the disposition of a sum of money)
    or b. The disposition of an object capable of delivery
  and 2. <u>Notice of the deposit is given to every party</u>
  and 3. <u>Leave of court is obtained</u>

b. Money paid into the court shall be deposited (pursuant to 28 USC 2041 and 2042, or any like statute).

c. The fund shall be deposited in an interest-bearing account, or a court approved investment.

# RULE 68: Offer of Judgment (Settlement)

a. <u>Pre-Trial Settlements</u>:
    1. **Definition:** Settlements must be offered at least <u>10 days</u> before the trial begins.
    2. A Defendant may serve upon an adverse party an offer to settle the case before trial.
    3. If the adverse party accepts the offer within <u>10 days</u>, either party may file the acceptance, and the clerk shall enter judgment.
    4. If the offer is not accepted, the offer shall be deemed withdrawn.
    5. A party rejecting an offer is not precluded from accepting subsequent offers.

6. If the judgment after trial is *equal to or less than* the settlement offer, the offeree has to pay the costs incurred after the offer was made.

b. Post-trial Settlements:

1. **Definition:** Settlement made after a party is found liable, yet before the amount of damages has been computed.

2. The party being held liable may make an offer to settle case before it proceeds further.

3. The offer must be made at least <u>10 days</u> before the hearing to determine the amount of damages due.

4. All other rules pertaining to pre-trial settlements apply to post-trial settlements.

# RULE 69: Execution

## (a) In General

1. A <u>Writ of Execution</u> shall be issued to enforce a judgment for the payment of money.

2. The procedure of the writ of execution shall be determined by the <u>state law</u> in which the district court sits (subject to applicable U.S. statutes).

3. The party entitled to judgment may obtain discovery from anyone, including the adverse party, in order to aid the execution.

## (b) Execution Against Certain Public Officers

1. Final judgment shall be satisfied as provided in U.S. statutes.

2. A Writ of Execution shall not be issued against the following type of public officers if the court has certified that the officer's actions fall within the relevant statutes:

a. Collector or other officer of revenue, pursuant to 28 USC §2006

b. An officer of Congress, pursuant to 2 USC §118

# Rule 70: Judgment For Specific Acts; Vesting Title

a. Scope - This rule applies if a party fails to comply with a judgment directing it to *either:*

    1. Execute a conveyance of land

  or 2. Deliver deeds or other documents

  or 3. Perform any other specific act

b. If the court appoints another person to do the act of the disobedient party:

    1. All costs of the act must be paid by the disobedient party.

  and 2. The act that the appointed person does has the same effect as if the disobedient party had done it.

c. Procedure:

    1. The party entitled to performance must file an application with the court

    2. Upon filing the application, the clerk shall issue a <u>Writ of Attachment or Sequestration</u> against the disobedient person's property in order to compel obedience to the judgment.

    3. The court may, *in proper cases,* hold the disobedient party in contempt.

    4. If real or personal property is within the court's district, the court may divest the title of any party and vest it in others entitled to it

    (Note: This has the same effect as a direct conveyance).

    5. When any order or judgment calls for delivery of possession, the entitled party may obtain a <u>Writ of Execution or Assistance</u>, upon application to the clerk.

# RULE 71: Process In Behalf Of And Against Non-Parties

Non-parties are subject to the same rules as parties, when non-parties are:

    1. Trying to obtain enforcement of an order

  or 2. Subject to enforcement of an order

# IX. SPECIAL PROCEEDINGS

## RULE 71A: Condemnation of Property (Eminent Domain)

**(a) Applicability of Other Rules** - Except as otherwise provided in these rules, the procedure for condemnation of property (eminent domain) is governed by the district court rules.

**(b) Joinder of Properties**
>π may join more than one piece of property in the same action, whether or not it is of different ownership or sought for the same use.

**(c) Complaint**
>(1) <u>Caption</u>
>>The complaint shall have a caption (pursuant to Rule 10(a)) except that the π shall name the property as Defendant, with the following details:
>>>a. Kind and quality of the property
>>>and b. Location of the property
>>>and c. At least one of the owners of some part or interest in the property

>(2) <u>Contents</u>
>>a. The complaint shall contain:
>>>1. A *short* and *plain* statement of authority for taking the property
>>>and 2. The use for which the property is being taken
>>>and 3. A description of the property sufficient for its identification
>>>and 4. The interests to be acquired
>>>and 5. A designation of the parties joined as owners or interest holders of each piece of property

b. <u>Who the π must join</u>:

    1. Once an action begins, the π only has to join people having or claiming an interest in the property whose names are then known.

    2. Before hearings begin to determine the compensation for the property, π must join <u>all</u> persons having or claiming an interest in the property.

        a. *Reasonable diligence* must be used to search records for interest holders.

        b. In determining the level of *reasonable diligence,* the court considers:

            1. The character and value of the property

        and 2. The interests to be acquired

        and 3. Those whose names have otherwise been learned

        c. All other owners may be made Defendants, designated as "unknown owners."

c. <u>Service</u>: Process must be served to all Defendants, even those added after the action begins, pursuant to Rule 71A(d).

d. <u>Answer</u>: Defendants may answer pursuant to Rule 71A(e).

e. <u>Deposit</u>: The court may order a distribution of a deposit as the facts warrant.

(3) <u>Filing</u> - The π must file a copy of the complaint (and additional copies upon request of the clerk or other parties) with

    a. The Court

    and b. The Clerk (for use of the Defendants)

## (d) Process

(1) <u>Delivering Notice</u>:

    a. After filing the complaint, the π shall deliver to the clerk joint or several notices directed to the Defendants (named in the complaint)

    b. If additional Defendants are added later, the π must give the clerk additional notices for them as well.

    c. The delivery of the notice to the clerk, and its service, have the same effect as a Rule 4 service of summons.

(2) <u>Form of Notice</u>:
  a. Each notice must include:
    1. The title of the action
   and 2. The court in which the action is pending
   and 3. The name of the Defendant to whom it is directed
   and 4. That the action is to condemn property
   and 5. A description of Defendant's property (sufficient for its identification)
   and 6. The interest to be taken
   and 7. The authority for taking it
   and 8. The use for which the property is to be taken
   and 9. The name of the $\pi$'s attorney
   and 10. An address within the district of the court, where the attorney may be served
   and 11. That the Defendant may serve an answer to $\pi$'s attorney within <u>20 days</u> after service (of the notice).
   and 12. That neglecting to answer constitutes consent to:
     a. The taking of the property
     b. The authority of the court to hear the action
     c. The authority of the court to fix the compensation
  b. The notice does not have to include a list of any other properties to be taken from the Defendants.
(3) <u>Service of Notice</u>
  (A) *Personal Service* (without copies of the complaint) - shall be made to Defendants residing in the U.S., at a known address (in accordance with Rule 4)
  (B) *Service by Publication*
   1. Publication notice may only be used if $\pi$'s attorney files a certificate stating:
     a. That he does not believe Defendant can be personally served
     b. That a *diligent inquiry* was conducted within the state in which the complaint was filed, and *either:*
       1. Defendant's residence cannot be ascertained
      or 2. If ascertained, it is beyond the territorial limits of personal service (as provided in this rule)

2. <u>Acceptable Notice</u> - π shall publish the notice once a
week for at least 3 weeks in one of the following:
   a. A local newspaper in which the property is
   located
   b. If no local publication exists, then in a newspaper
   having a general circulation where the
   property is located.
3. Prior to the last publication, a copy of the notice shall
also be mailed to a Defendant who cannot be
personally served under these rules, yet whose
address is ascertainable.
4. Unknown owners may be served by publication in a like
manner by a notice addressed to "unknown owners."
5. Service by publication is complete upon the date of the
last publication.
6. Proof of publication and mailing shall be made by
certificate of the π's attorney, with an attached copy
of the published notice, with the names and dates of
the newspaper marked thereon.
(4) <u>Return; Amendment</u> - Proof of service of the notice shall be made,
and amended notices (or proof of their service), shall be allowed (in
the manner provided under Rule 4(g)

## (e) **Appearance or Answer**

1. If the Defendant has no objection or defense to the taking of his
property, he shall serve a Notice of Appearance, designating the
property he has an interest in, so that he can receive notice of all
proceedings affecting it.
2. If the Defendant has an objection or defense to the taking of his
property:
   a. Defendant shall serve an answer within <u>20 days</u> of the
   service of π's original notice
   b. The answer shall:
      1. Identify the property in which the Defendant claims to
      have an interest
      and 2. State the nature and the extent of the interest claimed
      and 3. State all of Defendant's defenses and objections
   c. A Defendant waives all defenses and objections not stated
   in the answer (i.e. No other pleadings or motions asserting any
   additional defenses or objections are allowed)

3. At trial, the Defendant may present evidence as to the amount of *just compensation* to be paid for the property, whether or not he has previously appeared or answered.

## (f) Amendment of Pleadings

1. π is entitled to make amendments to his complaint if:
   a. It is done before the trial on the issue of compensation begins
   b. It does not result in a dismissal, pursuant to Rule 71A(i)
2. π need not serve a copy of the amendment, just a notice (pursuant to Rule 5(b)) to that it was filed, to any affected party who has appeared (and to any affected party who has not appeared (pursuant to 71A(d))).
3. π must give the clerk at least 1 copy of each amendment, and make an additional copy at the request of the clerk or a Defendant.
4. The Defendant may serve an answer to the amendments within 20 days of service (pursuant to Rule 71A(e)).

## (g) Substitution of Parties

1. If a Defendant dies, becomes incompetent, or transfers his property interest after he has already been joined, the court may order a substitution upon motion and notice of a hearing.
2. If the motion and notice of hearing are to be served upon new parties, service shall be made pursuant to Rule 71A(d)(3).

## (h) Trial

1. If the action involves Eminent Domain, and an act of Congress has appointed a special tribunal to determine the issue of just compensation, the tribunal will make the determination on that issue (and not the court).
2. If there is not an appointed tribunal, a party may demand a jury trial for the issue of just compensation (within the time allowed for answer, or a later time as the court may fix)
3. The court has discretion to refuse a jury trial and appoint its own 3-person commission to determine just compensation, because of either:
   a. The character, location, or quantity of the property to be condemned
   or b. Other reasons in the *interest of justice*

4. If a 3-member commission is appointed:
    a. The court may direct that no more than 2 additional persons serve as alternate commissioners to hear the case and replace commissioners who become disqualified, or are otherwise unable to perform their duties (before a decision is filed).
    b. Alternates who do not end up replacing regular commissioners will be discharged after the commission renders its final decision.
    c. <u>Examination of Commissioners</u>:
        1. Before appointing commissioners and alternates, the court must advise the parties of their identity and qualifications, and *may* permit the parties to examine them.
        2. Parties may not be allowed to suggest nominees.
        3. Each party has a right to object to an appointment, for *valid cause.*
    d. The commission shall have the same power as a master (pursuant to Rule 53).
5. Trial of all issues shall otherwise be by the court.

## (i) Dismissal of Action
(1) <u>As of Right</u>
    a. The π may dismiss an action by right and without a court order, if:
        1. No hearings on *just compensation* for the property have begun.
        2. π has not acquired title or any lesser interest, nor taken possession of the property.
    b. To dismiss the action, π must file a Notice of Dismissal, and include a brief description of the property.
(2) <u>By Stipulation</u>
    π may dismiss an action (in whole or in part) by stipulation or without a court order if:
        1. Both parties stipulate to the dismissal.
        2. Judgment has not been entered granting π title or any lesser interest or possession of the property.

(3) <u>By Order of the Court</u>
    a. The court may dismiss an action:
        1. Before the time that compensation has been
           determined and paid
        2. After hearings on *just compensation* begin
        3. If π has not acquired title or any lesser interest, or
           taken possession of the property
    b. If π has acquired title, possession, or an interest in the
       property, the court must award just compensation for the
       property that was taken.
    c. The court may at any time drop a Defendant who has been
       unnecessarily or improperly joined
(4) <u>Effect</u> - Dismissal is *without prejudice*, unless otherwise provided
    in a:
    a. Notice
    b. Stipulation of dismissal
    c. Order of the court

**(j) Deposit and Its Distribution**
    1. π <u>must</u> make any deposit of money required as a condition to the
       exercising of the power of eminent domain.
    2. π <u>may</u> make a deposit when permitted by statute (in such a case it helps
       speed up the process of ascertaining and distributing just compensation).
    3. If the deposit is *greater than* the final determination of just
       compensation, the court shall enter judgment against π, who
       must pay Defendant the balance (deficiency).
    4. If the deposit is *less than* the final determination of just
       compensation, the court shall enter judgment against the
       Defendant to return the balance (overpayment).

**(k) Condemnation Under a State's Power of Eminent Domain**
    1. These rules normally apply to actions involving the exercise of
       the power of eminent domain under the law of the state.
    2. If the state makes its own rules providing for trial of any issue by
       jury or for trial of the *"just compensation"* issue by the jury,
       commission, or both.

**(l) Costs** – Costs are not subject to Rule 54(d).

# RULE 72: Magistrates; Pretrial Orders

**(a) Nondispositive Matters**
1. Scope: This section applies when the district judge refers to a
    pre-trial matter which is <u>not</u> dispositive of a party's claim or
    defense to a <u>magistrate judge</u>.
2. The magistrate judge shall promptly hear and determine the
    pre-trial matter (as required by the trial judge) and, when appropriate,
    enter its disposition as a written order into the record.
3. Objections:
     a. If objections are not served and filed within <u>10 days</u> after the
        magistrate's order was served, a party loses its right to
        object to any error or disposition made by the magistrate.
     b. The district judge (to whom the case is assigned) shall consider any
        objections made (within a <u>10 day</u> time period) and *either:*
          1. Affirm the magistrate's order
       or 2. Reject it
       or 3. Modify a portion of it
     c. The district judge shall only reject or modify the magistrate's
        order if he finds that it is *either:*
          1. Clearly erroneous
       or 2. Contrary to law

**(b) Dispositive Motions and Prisoner Petitions**
1. Scope: This section applies when the district judge assigns a case
    to a magistrate judge *without the consent of the parties,* and:
        a. The matter is dispositive of a party's claim or defense
     or b. The matter involves a prisoner petition challenging the
        conditions of confinement
2. The magistrate judge shall promptly conduct such proceedings as
    are required.
3. The Record:
     **a. Required Material**:
          1. A record <u>must</u> be made of all evidentiary proceedings
            before the magistrate.
          2. The record must include a recommendation for
            disposition of the matter.

        b. <u>Optional Material</u>:
            1. A record <u>may</u> be made of any other proceedings the Magistrate deems necessary.
            2. A record may include proposed findings of fact, where appropriate.
        c. The clerk shall mail copies of the record to the parties.
    4. <u>Objections</u>:
        a. A party objecting to the recommended disposition of the magistrate shall *promptly* arrange for the transcription of all or part of the record (depending on what the parties agree on or the magistrate and district judge deem necessary).
        b. A party may serve and file *specific written* objections to the magistrate's recommendation within <u>10 days</u> of service of the magistrate's recommendation
        c. A party may respond to another party's objections within <u>10 days</u> of being served with the objection.
    5. <u>Judgment</u>:
        a. The district judge must make a *de novo* determination on any specific written objections.
        b. The district judge shall base its decision on:
            1. The magistrate record
            2. Additional evidence
        c. The district judge may either:
            1. Accept the magistrate's recommendation
        or 2. Reject it
        or 3. Modify it
        or 4. Receive further evidence
        or 5. Recommit the matter to the magistrate with instructions

# RULE 73: Magistrates; Trial by Consent and Appeal Options

**(a) Powers; Procedure**
    1. The magistrate's proceedings shall be conducted pursuant to 28 USC §636(c) when:
        a. A local rule or order by the district court gives the magistrate jurisdiction to hear the matter
     and b. All parties consent
    2. The magistrate may conduct a jury or non-jury trial, and conduct any or all proceedings in a civil case.

3. A record of the proceedings shall be made in accordance with 28 U.S.C. §636.

**(b) Consent**

1. When a magistrate has been given the jurisdiction to hear a civil trial, the clerk shall notify the parties of their opportunity to consent to it (as per 28 USC 636(c)).
2. If both parties consent, they shall execute and file either a joint form or separate forms, setting forth their mutual consent to a magistrate proceeding.
3. No judge or court official shall attempt to persuade or induce a party to consent to the magistrate referral.
4. No judge shall be informed of a party's response, unless all the parties consent.
5. The district judge may vacate a reference of a civil matter to a magistrate only in the following cases:
    a. On the judge's motion, only if *good cause* is shown
    or b. Under *extraordinary circumstances* shown by a party

**(c) Appeal** - Appeal from a magistrate judge's order shall be made in the appellate court, as it would if the district court had decided it.

# RULES 74, 75, and 76

These rules were abrogated to conform to the Federal Courts Improvement Act of 1996 which repealed the former provisions of 28 U.S.C. §636(c)(4) and (5), which enabled parties that had agreed to trial before a magistrate judge to also agree that appeals should be taken to the district court.

# X. DISTRICT COURTS AND CLERKS

## RULE 77: District Courts and Clerks

**(a) District Courts Always Open** - The district court shall be deemed *always open* for the purposes of:
   1. Filing any pleading or other proper paper
   and 2. Issuing and returning *mesne* and final process
   and 3. Making and directing all interlocutory motions, orders, and rules

**(b) Trials and Hearings; Orders in Chambers**
   1. All trials upon the merits shall be conducted in open court and in a regular and open court room
   2. All other acts and proceedings may be conducted by a judge in chambers:
       a. There is no need for clerk or other court official to be present
       b. The proceedings may be held outside of the district
   3. A hearing must be conducted within the district of the court, *unless:*
       a. All affected parties agree otherwise
       b. The hearing is *ex parte*

**(c) Clerk's Office and Orders by Clerk**
   1. The clerk's office will be open during regular business hours on all days except legal holidays and weekends.
   2. The clerk may grant all motions and applications for:
       a. Issuing mesne process
       and b. Issuing final process to enforce or execute a judgment
       and c. Entering default judgment
       and d. Other proceedings that do not require allowance or court order
   3. Upon *good cause* shown, the clerk's actions may be:
       a. Suspended
       or b. Altered
       or c. Rescinded

**(d) Notice of Orders of Judgments**
1. Immediately upon entry of judgment, the clerk shall:
    a. Serve a Notice of Entry of Judgment (by mail, pursuant to Rule 5)
        to each party not in default for failure to appear
    b. Make a note in the docket of the mailing
2. Lack of notice does not affect the time a party has to file an appeal, except as provided by the Federal Rules of Appellate Procedure, Rule 4(a).

# RULE 78: Motion Day

1. Each district court shall establish a regular schedule at intervals frequent enough for the prompt dispatch of business, in order to hear and dispose of motions requiring notice and hearings (unless local conditions make it impracticable).
2. A judge, upon reasonable notice, may, at any time or place, make an order for:
    a. Advancing actions
    b. The conduct and the hearing of actions
3. To expedite its business, the court may order that motions be submitted and determined upon brief statements, without an oral hearing.

# RULE 79: Books and Records Kept by the Clerk

**(a) Civil Docket**
1. The clerk shall keep a "civil docket" in which each civil action applicable to these rules is entered.
2. Actions shall be assigned consecutive file numbers.
3. The file number of each action shall be noted on the folio of the docket, where the first entry of the action is to be made.

4. The clerk shall chronologically enter into the docket all of the following:

    a. Papers filed with the clerk

and b. Process issued

and c. Returns made on process

and d. Appearances

and e. Orders

and f. Verdicts

and g. Judgments

5. Each entry shall be marked with:

    a. The file number (docket number) of the action

    b. The date of entry

6. Each entry shall be brief, yet detailed enough to show:

    a. The nature of each paper filed or writ issued

and b. The substance of each order or judgment and of the return showing execution of process.

7. The clerk shall enter the word "jury" on the folio if a trial by jury is properly ordered or demanded.

## (b) Civil Judgments and Orders

The clerk shall keep a correct copy of every:

1. Final judgment

and 2. Appealable order

and 3. Order affecting title to or lien on property

and 4. Any other order which the court may direct be kept

## (c) Indices; Calendars

1. An suitable index shall be maintained for:

    a. The civil docket

    b. Every civil judgment and order referred to in Rule 79(b)

2. A calendar shall be prepared for all actions ready for trial, which shall distinguish "jury actions" from "court actions."

## (d) Other Books and Records of the Clerk

The clerk shall keep such other books as may be required from time to time by the Director of the Administrative Office of the United States Courts with the approval of the Judicial Conference of the United States.

# RULE 80: Stenographer

**(a) Stenographer** - Abrogated, 1946

**(b) Official Stenographer** - Abrogated, 1946

**(c) Stenographic Report or Transcript as Evidence**
Testimony of a witness at a trial or hearing which is admissible as evidence and stenographically reported may be proved by the stenographic transcript if it is *certified* by the stenographer who reported it.

# *XI. GENERAL PROVISIONS*

## RULE 81: Applicability In General

### (a) To What Proceedings Applicable

(1) These rules do not apply to:
  a. Prize proceedings in admiralty (governed by 10 USC §7651-7681)
  b. Proceedings in bankruptcy
  c. Copyright proceedings (17 USC), except as directed by The
     U.S. Supreme Court
  d. Mental health proceedings in the district court for
     Washington D.C.

(2) These rules are applicable to the following proceedings:
  a. Admission to citizenship
  b. Quo Warranto (as long as not otherwise directed by a statute)
  c. Habeas Corpus - the writ of Habeas Corpus or order to show
     cause:
     1. Must be directed to the person having custody of the
        person detained.
     2. Must be returned within 3 days.
     3. If *good cause* shown, time limit may be extended to:
        a. 20 days
        or b. 40 days - if case is brought under 28 USC §2254

(3) These rules are applicable to proceedings for:
  a. *Arbitration* (9 USC) - applies only to the extent not provided
     for by other statutes
  b. *Boards of arbitration of railway labor disputes* - applies only
     to the extent not provided for by other statutes
  c. *Compelling the giving of testimony or production of
     documents according to a subpoena* - unless otherwise
     provided by statute or district court rules, or court order.

(4) <u>These rules do not alter methods prescribed by:</u>
  a. 7 USC §292 and 7 USC §499g(c) - proceedings to review orders of the Secretary of Agriculture,
  b. 15 USC §522 - proceedings to review orders of the Secretary of the Interior,
  c. 15 USC §715d(c) - proceedings to review orders of the Petroleum Control Boards, but *"the conduct of such proceedings in the district courts shall be made to conform to these rules as far as possible."*

(5) These rules <u>do not</u> alter the practice for proceedings involving the orders of the National Labor Relations Board (29 USC 159-160).

(6) These rules apply to proceedings for enforcement or review of compensation orders (under the Longshoreman's and Harbor Worker's Compensation Act, pursuant to 33 USC 918 and 921)

## (b) Scire Facias and Mandamus

1. The writs of <u>scire facias</u> and <u>mandamus</u> are abolished
2. Relief may now be obtained by appropriate action or motion prescribed by these rules

## (c) Removed Actions

1. These rules apply to civil actions removed to the U.S. district court (from state courts)
2. Re-pleading is not necessary unless the court so orders
3. If a Defendant has not answered before action is removed, he must answer or present an objection within the <u>later of</u>:
  a. <u>20 days</u> - after receipt of the initial pleadings (ex: complaint)
  b. <u>20 days</u> - after service of summons upon the initial pleadings filed
  c. <u>5 days</u> - after the filing of the petition for removal
4. A party will be entitled to a jury trial if:
  a. At the time of removal all necessary pleadings have been served
  and b. A demand is made within:
    1. For Petitioner: <u>10 days</u> after filing the petition for removal
    2. Other Parties: <u>10 days</u> after notice that the petition for removal has been served

5. If, before removal, a party made an appropriate demand for a jury according to state law, she need not make another demand (after case is remanded).
6. If state law does not require a demand to be made to obtain a jury trial, then the parties only have to make a demand in the district court if the court so orders (in its own discretion).
7. Failure to make a demand as directed constitutes a waiver by that party of the right to trial by jury.

## (d) District of Columbia; Courts and Judges.

(Abrogated Dec 29, 1948, eff Oct 20, 1949.)

## (e) Law Applicable

1. Whenever state law is referred to, and for purposes of this rule, **"state"** includes, if appropriate, the District of Columbia.
2. When the law of a state is referred to, the word **"law"** includes the statutes of that state and the state judicial decisions construing them.

## (f) Reference to Officer of the United States

Whenever reference is made to an <u>officer or agency of</u> the United States, the term "officer" includes
a. A District Director of Internal Revenue
or b. A former District Director or collector of Internal Revenue
or c. A Personal Representative of a deceased District Director
or d. A Director or Collector of Internal Revenue

# RULE 82: Jurisdiction and Venue

a. These rules shall not extend or limit the U.S. District Court's jurisdiction or venue.
b. An Admiralty or Maritime claim within the meaning of Rule 9(h) shall not be treated as a civil action for the purposes of 28 USC §1391-93.

# RULE 83: Rules By the District Courts

a. Each district court may make and amend rules governing its
    practice:
    1. By action of a majority of the judges
    2. After giving appropriate notice and an opportunity to
        comment
    3. As long as they are not inconsistent with these rules
b. A local rule shall take effect upon the date specified by the district
    court (and remain in effect until amended or abrogated).
c. Copies of the rules and amendments shall be made available to the
    public.
d. *"In all cases not provided for by rule, the district judges and
    magistrates may regulate their practice in any manner not
    inconsistent with these rules or those of the district in which
    they act."*

# RULE 84: Forms

"The forms contained in the Appendix of Forms are sufficient under
the rules and are intended to indicate the simplicity and brevity
of statements which the rules contemplate"

# RULE 85: Title

"These rules may be known and cited as the Federal Rules of Civil
Procedure."

# SELECTED STATUTES

## United States Code, Title 28 ("28 U.S.C.")

## §1291: Appellate Jurisdiction

The **appellate court** has jurisdiction of appeals from all final decisions of the district courts.

## §1292: Interlocutory Decisions

**(a)** The **appellate court** has the power to hear a case before final judgment when:

(1) <u>Injunctions</u>- There is an interlocutory order granting, continuing, modifying, refusing, or dissolving an injunction

(2) <u>Receivers</u> - There is an interlocutory order appointing a receiver (within the meaning of Rule 9)

(3) <u>Admiralty cases</u>

**(b) Judge's Request to Appeal**

1. If not included in (a), a district judge may request an interlocutory order appeal by *writing* to the appellate court within <u>10 days</u> after her order, if she believes there is a controlling question of law where there is substantial ground for difference of opinion, an appeal may *materially advance* the ultimate termination of the case.

2. The appellate court has discretion to accept such a request.

(c) U.S. appellate courts have **exclusive jurisdiction** of:

(1) Any case covered by §1295

and (2) Patent infringement cases which are final, except for an accounting (Where jurisdiction would otherwise lie in the Court of Appeals for the Federal Circuit)

**(d) Specific Issues:**

    i. The appellate court has discretion to take a case if:
        1. The application for appeal is made within <u>10 days</u> of an order is entered
    and 2. *Either:*
        a. The Chief Judge of the Court of International Trade issues a 256(b) interlocutory order.
        or b. The Chief Judge of the Court of Federal Claims issues a 798(b) interlocutory order.
        or c. Any judge of the Court of International Trade/Court of Federal Claims issues an interlocutory order.
    and 3. There is a *substantial ground* for difference of opinion on a controlling question of law.
    and 4. An immediate appeal may *materially advance* the termination of the suit.

    ii. <u>Applicability</u>
        (1) The above rules apply to the <u>Court of International Trade</u>.
        (2) The above rules apply to the <u>Court of Federal Claims</u>.
        (3) Proceedings <u>shall not</u> stay unless the district court or appellate court so orders.
        (4) <u>Motion To Transfer</u>
        (A) The appellate court has exclusive jurisdiction over all of the district court's <u>ordering</u>, <u>granting</u>, or <u>denying</u> of motions to transfer a case (pursuant to 28 USC §1631).
        (B) Actions <u>must</u> be stayed (put on hold) until <u>60 days</u> after the court has ruled upon a motion to transfer to the Court of Federal Claims. The time may be extended until after the appeal is decided (if an appeal is taken).

# §1331: Federal Questions

All civil actions *"arising under"* the U.S. Constitution, U.S. laws, or U.S. treaties have <u>original federal jurisdiction</u>.

## §1332: Diversity of Citizenship

(a) District courts have <u>original jurisdiction</u> if the matter in controversy is *greater than $75,000* is and is between *either:*

    (1) Citizens of different states

    or (2) Citizens of a state against citizens of foreign states or countries

    or (3) Citizens of different states, with additional parties from different states or countries

    or (4) Citizens of one state (or different states) against citizens of a foreign state acting as a π (pursuant to 28 USC §1603(a))

(b) If the final judgment is $75,000 or less, the court may impose costs on π.

(c) **§1332/§1441 "Citizenship"**

    1. <u>Corporate Citizenship</u> is considered both:

        a. The corporation's state of incorporation

        and b. The corporation's principal place of business

    2. <u>Insurance Company's Citizenship</u> is:

        a. Its state of incorporation

        and b. Its principal place of business

        and c. The state of the insured person (customer) if the insurance company is not joined as a Defendant.

    3. <u>Executors/Trustees</u> are citizens of the state of the decedent/beneficiary, with regard to related claims.

    4. <u>Aliens</u> are citizens of the state where they are domiciled (as per §1332(a)), if they reside there with the intention of becoming a <u>permanent resident</u> of U.S.

# *Interpleader Statutes*

## §1335: Interpleader
("Statutory Interpleader" - minimal diversity allowed)

(a) The district court has original jurisdiction over a civil action of interpleader if:

    (1) Subject Matter Jurisdiction exists:

        a. The controversy is *greater than or equal to $500*

and b. **Minimal Diversity**: At least 2 parties need diversity of citizenship (not all)

and (2) "Stakeholder" posts a bond (or deposits the property in the court)

(b) Interpleader may take place, although

    1. There is no common origin among the titles or claims of the conflicting claimants

    or 2. The actions are not identical, but are adverse and independent actions.

# §1397: Interpleader Venue

A §1335 interpleader action may be brought in a judicial district where *greater than or equal to* 1 <u>claimant</u> resides.

# §1367: Supplemental Jurisdiction
**(Over subsequent parties or actions)**

**(a) "Supplemental Jurisdiction"** - includes jurisdiction over any claims *related* to the claims in an action which form the *same case or controversy* (including joinder or intervention of claims).

**(b) Supplemental-Diversity Jurisdiction** - When courts have Subject Matter Jurisdiction based only on diversity, **complete diversity** <u>must</u> be continued for all counter-claims against third parties.

**(c) Court's Discretion** - A Court may decline Supplemental Jurisdiction if:

    1. The claim raises a novel or complex issue of state law

    or 2. The claim is *"substantially"* predominant over the original (federal) claim.

    or 3. The court dismissed all claims having Subject Matter Jurisdiction

    or 4. Exceptional circumstances compel the federal court to decline jurisdiction.

**(d) Statute of Limitations** – for a supplemental claim that is dismissed (or any other claim in the same action that is dismissed at the same time or after) is tolled while:

    1. The supplemental claim is pending

or 2. For a period of <u>30 days</u> after its dismissal *unless* state law provides for a longer tolling period.

**(e) "State"** includes the District of Columbia, Puerto Rico, and any other U.S. territory.

# *Venue Statutes*

## §1391: Venue

(a) **Diversity Case:** If a case has federal jurisdiction based <u>solely</u> on diversity, it may be brought:

    1. In the district court where <u>any</u> Defendant resides, if all Defendants reside in same state.

    or 2. In the district court where *<u>substantial</u>* <u>events</u> or <u>property</u> is located.

    or 3. If no other district can hear the case, then it may be heard wherever <u>all</u> Defendants are subject to personal jurisdiction at the commencement of the action (if no such place is available, the parties must bring separate suits).

(b) **Jurisdiction Not Based Solely on Diversity:** Suits involving a **federal question** (as defined in §1331) may be brought:

    1. In the district court where <u>any</u> Defendant resides, if all Defendants reside in same state

    or 2. In the district court where *<u>substantial</u>* <u>events</u> or <u>property</u> is located

    or 3. If no other district is available, then the suit may be brought wherever <u>any</u> one Defendant may be found.

(c) **Corporate Venue:**

    1. Wherever a corporation is subject to personal jurisdiction at commencement of the action (any district where "contacts" would give the corporation personal jurisdiction (under the "minimum contacts test")).

    2. If none available, look to the district with the most *"significant"* contacts.

    3. If there is no one particular district in the state in which the company has enough contacts for personal jurisdiction, but the state <u>as a whole</u> "qualifies" (under the "minimum contacts test"), the entire state is considered to have personal jurisdiction over the Defendant corporation.

**(d) Venue of an Alien:** An alien may be sued in any district.

**(e) Venue for an Officer or Employee of the U.S.**
    (1) Where a <u>Defendant resides</u> (if all Defendants reside in the same state).
    (2) Where *substantial* <u>events</u> or <u>property</u> exist
    (3) If no real property is involved, then where the $\pi$ <u>resides</u>

**(f) Venue for a Suit Against a Foreign State** (as defined in §1603(a)):
    1. Where *substantial* <u>events</u> or <u>property</u> exist
    2. Where the vessel or cargo is situated
    3. Wherever the agency is licensed to do business (or actually does business)

# §1392: Multiple Districts

If Defendants reside or have property located in more than 1 district, $\pi$ can bring the action in any of those districts.

# §1404: Change of Venue

(a)  i. Change of venue may be made for the following reasons:
      1. Convenience of parties
    or 2. Convenience of witnesses
    or 3. *"In the interest of justice"*
  ii. A district may transfer a case to any other district where the case *may have been brought.*

or **(b)** Both parties may consent to change venue (subject to the court's discretion)

**(c)** A district court may order any civil action to be tried at any place within the division in which it is pending.

**(d) Definitions**:
    1. **"District Court"** includes U.S. District Court for the District of the Canal Zone.
    2. **"District"** includes the territorial jurisdiction of that court.

## §1406: Waiver of Venue

(a) If venue is wrong, the district court may:
1. Dismiss the case
or 2. Transfer the case to an appropriate district

(b) Even if a party does not make a timely and sufficient objection to venue, jurisdiction <u>will not</u> be destroyed (See Rule 12 for bringing a motion for improper venue).

# *Removal Statutes*

## §1441: Cases That Can Be Removed to Federal Court

**(a) Removal From State Court by Defendant**
Whenever federal courts have <u>original jurisdiction</u>, a case may be removed from the state court <u>by the Defendant</u> (but not by the π) to the appropriate federal court in the district of original state forum.

**(b) Removable Subject Matters:**
1. <u>Any</u> **federal question** case may be removed without regard to residence of the parties
2. **Diversity cases** may be removed as long as <u>any</u> Defendant is not a citizen of the present forum.

**(c) Joinder of Cause** - When an independent federal question is joined with a non-federal subject matter, the court may choose to either:
1. Split the matters and hear only the federal element of case
or 2. Hear the entire case
or 3. Remand matters where state law predominates

**(d) Foreign State Defendant** - When a π sues a foreign state, the case may be removed by the foreign state (and tried without a jury; limitations of §1446(b) may be enlarged).

**(e) No Need to Re-file:** The federal court to which a case is removed may still hear a case that the state court had no jurisdiction over (the case need not be dismissed and re-filed in federal court).

# §1445: Non-Removable Cases

The following cases <u>may not</u> be removed:
    (a) Railroad cases (pursuant to 45 USC §51-60)
    (b) Common carriers if the amount is *greater than or equal to* $10,000 (pursuant to 45 USC §11707)
    (c) State Worker's Compensation law cases

# §1446: Procedure for Removal

(a) **Filing** - Must file pursuant to Rule 11, with a:
    (1) Short statement of the grounds for removal
    (2) Copy of process and pleadings
    (3) Copy of orders served upon the Defendant

(b) **Limitations**
    1. Must file within <u>30 days</u> after (the shorter of):
        a. Defendant's receipt of $\pi$'s initial pleadings
        b. Service of the summons, if pleadings are not required to be served
    2. If $\pi$ amends the pleadings (making the case removable) the Defendant may file for removal within <u>30 days</u> after $\pi$'s amended pleadings are filed and delivered.

\* \* \*

(d) Promptly after filing, the Defendant shall give <u>written notice</u> to all parties and shall file a copy with the clerk. Once the state court is notified, the state court *automatically* loses control.

(e) If a Defendant has actual custody of process issued by the state court, the district court shall issue its <u>writ of habeas corpus</u>, and the marshal shall take the Defendant into his custody, and deliver a copy of the writ to the clerk of the state court.

# §1447: Procedure After Removal

(a) A court may do "anything" to bring all parties before it.

(b) <u>District Court may</u>:
> 1. Require the party asking for removal to file all records of the state court proceedings with the district court clerk.

> and 2. Cause all records to be brought before it by having the state court issue a <u>Writ of Certiorari</u>.

(c) **Motion to Remand** (for a defect in removal procedure)
> 1. A motion to remand (back to state court) may be made by $\pi$.
> 2. The motion must be within <u>30 days</u> of the §1446 filing of notice.
> 3. If the district court lacks subject matter jurisdiction at any time before judgment, the case can be remanded to state court.
> 4. Orders remanding a case back to the state may require payment of expenses associated with removal.
> 5. The state court shall proceed with the case once the district court clerk mails a certified copy of the order of remand.

(d) An order to remand is not appealable (unless removed pursuant to §1443).

(e) If, after removal, the $\pi$ joins other Defendants that destroy subject matter jurisdiction (i.e. no more complete diversity), the court may:
> 1. Deny the joinder
> or 2. Remand the case to state court

# §1651: Writ of Mandamus

> 1. A <u>Writ of Mandamus</u> will allow immediate appeal, contrary to all laws (i.e. the judge may act beyond normal powers).
> 2. The Supreme Court (and all other courts established by Act of Congress) may issue all writs necessary or appropriate in their jurisdiction.

# *A*PPENDIX

# RULE 4: Process
**(Pre-1993 Amendments)**

**(a) Issuing the Summons:**
1. π files complaint with the clerk
2. The clerk issues a summons and delivers it to the π or π's attorney
3. π or π's attorney is responsible to deliver the summons and complaint to the Defendant.

**(b) Summons Form:** Must be signed by the clerk, with the seal of court, the name of the court, the names of the parties, π and π's attorney's name, address, and the time for Defendant to appear before <u>default judgment</u> can be entered.

**(c) Service**:
(1) Other than a subpoena or summons and complaint shall be served by a U.S. Marshal or a specially appointed person.

(2) <u>Summons and Complaint</u>
   (A) May be served by:
      (i) Anyone 18 years old or more
   and (ii) Any non-party to the suit
   (B) π may request a U.S. Marshal or specially appointed agent to serve, but only if:
      (i) On behalf of a party in a <u>forma pauperis</u> suit
      (ii) On behalf of the U.S. or a U.S. agency
      (iii) By special court order - to effectuate a particular action
   (C) <u>Service</u> - may either be done:
      (i) Pursuant to state law
      (ii) By mailing 1st class or postage prepaid:
         a. A copy of the summons
     and b. 2 copies of a notice and acknowledgement Form 18-A
     and c. Postage prepaid return envelope
      iii. If not returned within <u>20 days</u>, must use:

1. Personal service (4(c)(2)(A))
2. U.S. Marshal service (4(c)(2)(B))

(D) If the Defendant does not return form 18-A within <u>20 days</u>, the Defendant shall pay for personal service (unless *good cause* is shown)

(E) Notice of Acknowledgement of Receipt of Summons by mail must be made under oath.

(3) Courts may freely order:

a. 4(c)(2)(b) U.S. Marshal service for a summons or complaint

or b. 4(c)(1) service all other process (i.e. for non-summons and complaint)

**(d) Person to be Served** - π shall furnish someone to serve <u>both</u> the summons and complaint together in one of the following ways:

(1) <u>Personal Service</u>

a. *Personal:* To actual individual

b. *Abode:* To someone (of suitable age) residing at the Defendant's home

c. *Substitute:* To an authorized agent

(2) <u>Infant/Incompetent</u> - According to state law

(3) <u>Corporation/Business</u> - Deliver to a general agent, officer, manager, or authorized agent

(4) <u>United States</u> - Deliver to the U.S. Attorney for the district, with certified mailing to the government officer/agent

(5) <u>To a U.S. Agency</u> - Certified mail to an officer/agency (if it is a U.S. corporation, see Rule 4(d)(3))

(6) <u>State/Municipal Corporations</u> - Deliver to the CEO of the corporation, <u>or</u> according to state law.

**(e) Service Upon Out-Of-State Defendants**

1. When a federal statue exists, it may be used (otherwise service is done according to these rules)

or 2. A state rule may be used if it provides:

a. For service to out-of-state citizens

b. An In-Rem/Long-Arm statute clause

**(f) Territorial Limits of Effective Service**
　　1. May be served anywhere within the district court's state limits
　　2. Limits extended by:
　　　　(a) Authorized Statutes
　　　　(b) Federal Rules of Civil Procedure
　　3. May be extended <u>100 miles</u> from the district court if the
　　　　Defendant is a third party or a party to a counterclaim.
　　4. For subpoena service within the territorial limits, see Rule 45.

**(g) Return:**
　　1. Proof of service must be filed within the time the person served
　　　　may respond.
　　2. Service can be proven with *either:*
　　　　a. <u>An affidavit</u>
　　or b. Return <u>of Form 18-A</u>, if mail service was used
　　3. Failure to make proof of service does not affect the validity of
　　　　the service.

**(h) Amendment:**　The court may allow any process or proof of service to
be amended if it would not *materially prejudice* a party.

**(i) Service in a Foreign Country:**
　　(1) <u>Manner</u> - Prescribed by:
　　　　A. The foreign country
　　or B. A foreign authority in response to a Letter Rogatory,
　　　　　　when service is *reasonably calculated* to give actual
　　　　　　notice
　　or C. Personal delivery
　　or D. Registered mail
　　or E. As directed by the court

　　(2) <u>Return</u> - By foreign law or as per U.S. Federal Rules of return
　　　　(Rule 4(g))
　　　　(Note: It is the power of the legislature to extend jurisdiction further)

## (j) Time Limit for Service

    1. If service is not made within <u>12 Days</u> of filing, the case will either be Automatically dismissed (without prejudice), *either*:

        a. Upon the court's initiative (with notice to the parties)

       or b. Upon motion

    2. The court may extend the service period if:

        a. The $\pi$ shows *good cause*

       or b. Service was made to a foreign country

# *Discovery Rules*
### (Pre-1993 Amendments)

## RULE 26: General Provisions Governing Discovery

**(a) Discovery Methods** - May be obtained by <u>one or more</u> of the following:
> 1. <u>Depositions</u> - oral or written
> 2. <u>Interrogations</u> - written
> 3. <u>Production of Documents</u> - or things
> 4. <u>Permission to Enter</u> - upon land or other property for inspection and other purposes
> 5. <u>Examinations</u> - physical and mental
> 6. <u>Requests for Admission</u>

**(b) Discovery Scope and Limits**
> (1) *In General*
>> a. Parties may obtain "discovery" regarding any matter:
>>> 1. Not privileged
>>> 2. Relevant to the subject of the action or any party in the action
>>
>> b. If the information sought appears *reasonably calculated* to lead to the discovery of admissible evidence, there can be <u>no</u> grounds for objection to obtaining them.
>> c. Use of discovery limited if:
>>> i. Discovery sought is:
>>>> a. Unreasonably cumulative or duplicative
>>>> or b. Obtainable from a more convenient or less expensive source
>>>
>>> ii. The party seeking discovery has an ample opportunity to obtain the information sought elsewhere
>>> iii. The discovery is unduly burdensome or expensive in comparison to:
>>>> a. Needs of the case
>>>> or b. Amount in controversy
>>>> or c. Limitations on parties' resources
>>>> or d. Importance of issues at stake in the litigation

d. The court may act on its own initiative or pursuant to a motion to limit discovery.

(2) *Insurance Agreements*

    a. Obtainable if the insurance company may be liable to:

        1. Satisfy all or part of the judgment

        2. Indemnify party for judgment

        3. Reimburse for payments on the judgment

    b. Information concerning the insurance agreement itself is not admissible in evidence.

(3) *Trial Preparation: Materials (Work-Product Rule)*

    a. Disclosure: A party may obtain discovery gathered by another party only upon a showing that the party:

        1. Has a *substantial need* for the materials to prepare her case

        2. Cannot obtain the *"substantial equivalent"* of the materials without *"undue hardship"*

    b. Disclosure is limited to the materials themselves. Courts will protect the other party's conclusions, theories of recovery, strategies, etc.

    c. If a party *previously* made a statement concerning the action or subject matter, he does not have to present a new one when obtaining the other party's materials:

        1. If the other party denies materials:

            a. The party seeking discovery may move for a court order to obtain the other party's materials.

        and b. The party seeking discovery may apply for expenses incurred in relation to the motion (as per Rule 37(a)(4)).

        2. A **"previously made statement"** is:

            a. A written statement signed or adopted by the person making it

            b. A recorded transcript or recording of an oral statement by the person making the "showing"

(4) *Trial Preparation; Obtaining Expert Opinions:*
    (A) ***Experts to be used****:*
        (i) A party may request the following information with respect to the other party's <u>expert testimony</u> by serving interrogatories on the other party:
            a. Identity of each expert witness
            b. Subject matter each witness will testify to
            c. Substance of facts and opinions the expert is expected to testify about
            d. Summary of the grounds for each of the expert's conclusions or opinions
        (ii) Upon motion, the court may order further discovery by other means (other than interrogatories) subject to restrictions of scope, expenses, etc.
        iii. <u>Fees</u>: The court <u>may</u> require a party to reimburse a portion of the other party's expert testimony expenses.
    (B) ***Experts not to be used****:*
        i. A party may get another party's expert information used to prepare for litigation (but not to be used as a witnesses for trial) if he can prove:
            (1) *Exceptional Circumstances* - it is impractical to obtain facts on same subject by other means
           or (2) He is entitled to the information under Rule 35(b).
        ii. <u>Fees</u>: The court <u>must</u> charge a party a *reasonable* portion of the other party's expert testimony expense.

**(c) Protective Orders:**
    1. Upon <u>motion</u> and a showing of *good cause,* a court may make any order *which justice requires* to protect any party from:
        a. annoyance
        or b. embarrassment
        or c. oppression
        or d. undue burden or expense

    2. Controls that a court may use to protect parties include *one or more of the following*:
        a. That discovery not be had

b. Discovery may be had only on *specified terms and conditions*

c. Discovery be had by a *certain method*

d. Discovery scope be limited to *certain matters,* prohibiting inquiry into other matters

e. Discovery be conducted in the privacy of a court designee

f. Sealed depositions only to be opened by court order

g. Trade secrets/confidentiality not to be disclosed, or disclosed in a specified manner

h. Parties file simultaneous specified documents or information in sealed envelopes to be opened with a court order

## (d) Sequence and Timing of Discovery

Methods of discovery may be used in any order, unless the court grants a motion, based on:

1. Resulting injustice

or 2. Inconvenience of the parties or witnesses

or 3. Delay to the other party's discovery

## (e) Supplementation of Responses

When a party responds to a discovery request, he is <u>obligated</u> to supplement it with newly acquired information (obtained after testifying) if:

1. <u>The questions are related to the identity or location of</u>:

A. People with knowledge of discovery matters

B. Expert Witnesses expected to be called at trial:

1. Identity

2. Subject matter of expected testimony

3. Substance of expert's expected opinion

or 2. <u>The questions are related to Incorrect Testimony</u>:

A. The party knows the response was incorrect *when made*

B. The party knows the response is *no longer* correct (though ok when made) and failure to amend his testimony is "in substance" a *knowing concealment*

or 3. <u>It is specifically requested</u>

A. By order of Court

B. By agreement of parties

C. By requests for supplementation of prior responses (prior to trial)

**(f) Discovery Conference:**
 i. The court may order a conference on its own initiative or by motion.
 ii. <u>Requirements of a Motion for a Discovery Conference</u> - If the following requirements are met, the court must order a conference:
   (1) Statement of the issues [as they then appear to be]
  and (2) A proposed plan/schedule of discovery
  and (3) Proposed discovery limitations
  and (4) Proposed discovery orders
  and (5) Attorney's Affirmation
    a. That made reasonable effort to reach an agreement with other side concerning the motion matters
    b. Good faith in framing a discovery plan
 ii. <u>Motion Rules</u>
  a. Notice of motion proposed served on all parties
  b. Objections/additions of motion shall be served no more than <u>10 days</u> after the original motion was served.

 iii. <u>Outcome of Conference:</u>
  a. Court shall tentatively identify the issues for discovery purposes
  b. Establish a plan/schedule for discovery
  c. Other Matters - such as allocation of expenses, management of discovery action.
  d. Note: orders may be altered/amended when justice requires.

 iv. Court may combine discovery conference with pre-trial conference (Rule 16).

**(g) Signing of Discovery Requests, Responses, and Objections**
 1. Must be signed by at least one attorney (or the party if its not represented) to be valid (recognized by court).
 2. <u>Signature</u> - a signature certifies that:
  a. The signer read the request, response, and objection
  b. To the *best of his knowledge*, the information is:
   1. Formed after a <u>*reasonable inquiry*</u>
   2. Consistent with good faith and existing law
   3. Not used for inappropriate purposes – such as harassment, delay, increased costs of litigation

4. Not unreasonable/unduly burdensome/expensive in light of case

2. If not signed, the discovery will be <u>Stricken</u> (unless signed promptly after the omission is brought to the party's attention)

3. Appropriate sanctions (such as in Rule 11) will be made for violation of this rule, either by:
   a. Court's own initiative
   b. Motion by opposing side

# RULE 37: <u>Sanctions for Failure to Make or Cooperate in Discovery</u>

**(a) Motion for Order Compelling Discovery**
   (1) <u>Appropriate Court</u>
      a. Where the action is pending
      b. Where the deposition is pending, if the deponent is not a party

   (2) <u>Motion</u>
      a. If the deponent refuses to answer, the party may make a motion for an <u>order compelling an answer</u>
      b. If court denies motion, it may grant deponent a <u>protective order</u> (as per Rule 26(c))

   (3) <u>Evasive or Incomplete Answer</u> - considered a failure to answer

   (4) <u>Award of Expenses of Motion</u>
      a. If the objection is not substantially justified, the party/deponent must pay reasonable fees spent to make the motion, but only if motion is **granted**.
      b. If the motion is not substantially justified, the party making the motion must pay reasonable fees spent to oppose the motion, if motion is **denied.**
      c. If the motion is denied in part and granted in part, expenses may be reasonably apportioned.

**(b) Failure to Comply with Order**

(1) <u>Sanctions by Court in District where Deposition is Taken</u> - Failure to be sworn or answer is considered contempt in that court.

(2) <u>Sanctions by Court in District where Action is Pending</u> - The court may:
>> (A) Conclude that matters sought to be discovered by a party are in that party's favor
>> (B) Refuse to allow the disobedient party to support or oppose designated claims or defenses
>> (C) Render a default judgment or strike a pleading
>> (D) Hold disobedient person in contempt of court (unless for a physical/mental examination)
>> (E) Unless the court finds the disobedience *substantially justified* the opposing party must pay *reasonable* attorneys fees resulting from the disobedience.

## (c) Expenses on Failure to Admit
If a party refuses to admit to the authenticity of a document, and the other party proves its authenticity, the other party may impose fees spent to prove validity, unless:
> 1. Request objectionable (as per Rule 36(a))
> or 2. Admission sought was of no *substantial* importance
> or 3. The party failing to admit had *reasonable* grounds to believe he would prevail on that matter
> or 4. Other *good cause* shown

## (d) Failure to Attend a Deposition, Serve Answers, or Respond to Production Requests - subjects a party to Rule 37(b) sanctions above.

## (e) Failure to Participate in Framing a Discovery Plan
If no good faith effort is made to agree on a plan, reasonable attorney fees to bring the plan to court will be imposed.

Relevance, R26(b)(1).
Work product,
  R26(b)(3), R33(b),
  R36(a).
Sequence of, R26(d).
Signing of, R26(g).
Stipulations regarding,
  R29.
Subpoenas, See Subpoena.
Supplementation of
  responses, R26(e).

**DISMISSAL**
Class actions, R23(e).
Involuntary, R41(b).
Motion to dismiss,
  R12(b).
Voluntary,
  Actions, R41.

**DISTRICT COURTS**
Jurisdiction, See
  Subject-Matter
  Jurisdiction.
Open, R77(a).
Venue, See Venue.

**DIVERSITY
  JURISDICTION**
Alienage, 28 USC 1332.
Corporate citizenship, 28

USC 1332(c)(1).
General provision, 28
  USC 1332.
Interpleader, 28 USC
  1335.
Jurisdictional amount, 28
  USC 1332, 28 USC
  1335(a).
Removal, 28 USC 1441.
Venue, 28 USC 1391(a),
  28 USC 1397.

**ENFORCEMENT OF
  JUDGMENTS**
Discovery, R69(a).
Execution, R69, R70.
Money judgment, R69.
Non-money judgment,
  R70.
Nonparties, R71.
Supplementary pleadings,
  R69(a).

**ERIE DOCTRINE**
See State Law in Federal
  Court.

**ERROR**
Harmless, See Harmless
  Error.
Plain, See Plain Error.

# INDEX

**ORDERS**
See also Judgment.
Pretrial, R16(e).
Temporary restraining, see
Injunctions.

**PARTIES**
Capacity, R9(a), R17.
Indispensable, R19(b).
Involuntary plaintiff,
R19(a).
Joinder of, see Joinder.
Necessary, R19(a).
Proper, R17, R20(a).
Real party in interest,
R17(a).
Substitution of, R25.
United States, see United
States as Party.

**PATENTS**
Appeal, 28 USC 1292(c),
28 USC 1295(a).
Stay of judgment, R62(a).
Subject-matter
jurisdiction, 28 USC
1338.
Venue, 28 USC 1400(b).

**PERSONAL
JURISDICTION**
Defenses to, R12.

Nonpersonal actions,
R4(e), R13(a).
Removed cases, 28 USC
1447(a), 28 USC
1448.
Service of process, R4,
R6(e).
Summons, R4.
Sureties, R65.1.
United States as
defendant, R4,
R15(c).

**PLEADINGS**
Alternative, R8, R18.
Amendment of, see
Amendment.
Counts, R8(e), R10(b).
Defenses, see Defenses.
Form of, R10, R25(d).
General rules, R8.
Nonjoinder reasons,
R19(c).
Removed cases, R81(c).
Sanctions, R11.
Signing of, R11, R23.1,
R66.
Special matters, R9.
Supplemental, R13(e),
R15(d).
Types of, R7.
Answer, see Answer.

Removed cases, R81(c).
Seizure for security, R64.
Service of process, R4.
Stay of judgment, R62(f).

**STATUTE OF
LIMITATIONS**
See Limitations.

**STAYS**
Judgment,
General provision, R62.
Proceedings,
Lower court, 28 USC
1292.

**SUBJECT-MATTER
JURISDICTION**
Admiralty, 28 USC 1333.
Alienage, 28 USC 1332.
Courts of appeals', see
Courts of Appeals.

**SUBJECT-MATTER
JURISDICTION**
Defenses to, R12.
Diversity, general, 28
USC 1332.
Effect of rules on, R82.
Federal question, general,
28 USC 1331.
Interpleader, statutory, 28

USC 1335.
Jurisdictional amount,
Commerce cases, 28
USC 1337, 28 USC
1445(b).
Diversity cases, 28 USC
1332.
Interpleader cases,
statutory, 28 USC
1335(a).
Sanction, 28 USC
1332(b), 28 USC
1337(b).
Mandamus, R81(b).
Pleading of, R8(a), R9(e).
Removal, see Removal.
Supplemental, 28 USC
1367.

**SUBPOENA**
Duces tecum, R45.
General provision, R45.
Government, R81(a)(3).
Service, R4(f), R45(b).

**SUBSTITUTION**
Amendment of pleadings,
see Amendment.
Parties,
Trial court, R17(a),
R25.